General Physics Laboratory

TOMOYUKI NAKAYAMA

Tokyo-Kyogakusha Co., Ltd.
Tokyo, Japan

Published by Tokyo-Kyogakusha Co., Ltd.
3-10-5 Koishikawa, Bunkyo-ku,
Tokyo 112-0002, Japan

Copyright © 2017 by Tomoyuki Nakayama

All rights reserved. No part of this publication may be reproduced, stored in a retrieval system, or transmitted, in any form or by any means, without the prior permission of the publisher.

ISBN978-4-8082-2078-5

Printed in Japan

*To my parents Yoshihiro and Haruko Nakayama,
whose abiding faith in me and continuous support have enabled me
to keep striving for my own achievements.*

Preface

This book is intended as lab manuals for Physics Experiment I & II, general physics courses offered to freshman students at Tokyo Institute of Technology (Tokyo Tech); it is originally written for the GSEP (Global Scientists and Engineers Program) students during the academic year of 2016.

The GSEP is a newly established undergraduate program administered by Tokyo Tech for international students aspiring to be scientists or engineers with global perspectives. Applicants to this program do not need to have proficiency in Japanese, for the institute has allotted an extra budget to hire English-speaking instructors for all the required courses. Unfortunately, laboratory courses are not mandatory at Tokyo Tech, and many of the laboratory courses, including chemistry labs and biology labs, were unable to accommodate these international students without sufficient budget and preparation period. However, in my opinion, acquiring basic laboratory skills and data analysis techniques are an integral part of undergraduate science education, and I believed that it was our responsibility to offer at least one laboratory course to the incoming GSEP students. Since I had engaged myself in college-level physics education in the United States for more than eight years, including experience in developing a newly offered studio-type physical science course (a lecture-lab combined course taught by a single instructor in a small classroom), I decided to take care of the first batch of the GSEP students by myself and to establish a system to accommodate international students every year without an additional budget.

Preparing a full-fledged textbook was one of the major parts of the project. For Japanese students, Tokyo Tech not only offers a textbook (by Fumio Kakimoto, Kenji Ema *et al.*), but also lab manuals that can be accessed from computers in the laboratory. This book is carefully designed so that the essential pieces of information written in the Japanese textbook and the laboratory manuals are all included. The Japanese textbook was written by multiple authors, so each chapter is written in a different style and format. I stuck to a single format so that students can get used to the book's style quickly and focus on grasping the content itself. Also, I often explained the background theories of the experiments more in details and added some comprehension questions to help instructors access their students' understandings further.

To write this book, I first referred to numerous lab manuals used in English-speaking countries for each laboratory theme to acquire diverse points of view on the theme and deeper understanding of the laboratory, and then attempted to explain things on my own words, while being cautious not to miss crucial bits of information written in the Japanese textbook and manuals.

On the other hand, I need to admit that this textbook is still minimal. This book only contains 12 experiments out of 16 available ones in the laboratory. Chapters on measurement and error analysis are not included. Hence this book currently serves exclusively the GSEP students at Tokyo Tech. To make this book more versatile and appealing to a wider range of readers, a revision, which I intend to get done within a few years, is awaited.

I would really like to thank many people that have made this publication possible. I appreciate Toshiyuki Kikuchi who provided me with a favorable environment to concentrate on writing this book, Kenji Ema who generously agreed to let me use the figures he had prepared, Hidekazu Tanaka who gave me an opportunity to take care of the inaugural class of the GSEP, and Toshimasa Fujisawa who has positively fostered the publication, just to name a few. Lastly I would like to show my acknowledgment to the first batch of the GSEP students for their courage to enroll into a brand new program and diligence with which they all successfully completed the physics lab courses. I hope the future prosperity of the GSEP students and the GESP itself, and that this book will be of some help for this purpose.

Tomoyuki Nakayama

Ookayama, Tokyo
March 2017

Contents

1 Angular Momentum   **1**
- 1.1 Introduction 1
- 1.2 Objective 1
- 1.3 Theory 1
  - 1.3.1 Equation of Translational Motion 2
  - 1.3.2 Torque 2
  - 1.3.3 Angular Momentum 4
  - 1.3.4 Moment of Inertia and the Newton's 2nd Law for Rotation . . 5
  - 1.3.5 Parallel-Axis Theorem 6
- 1.4 Apparatus 7
- 1.5 Procedure 7
  - 1.5.1 Spinning Bicycle Wheel 7
  - 1.5.2 Rotating Stool and Dumbbells 8
  - 1.5.3 Gyroscope 9
- 1.6 Comprehension Questions 11

2 Young's Modulus   **12**
- 2.1 Introduction 12
- 2.2 Objective 12
- 2.3 Theory 13
  - 2.3.1 Young's Modulus 13
  - 2.3.2 Flexure of a Beam and Young's Modulus 13
  - 2.3.3 Optical Lever 16
- 2.4 Apparatus 17
  - 2.4.1 Young's Modulus Apparatus 17
  - 2.4.2 Telescope 18
  - 2.4.3 Others 18
- 2.5 Procedure 19
  - 2.5.1 Setup 19
  - 2.5.2 Adjustment of Telescope 20
  - 2.5.3 Measurement 20
  - 2.5.4 Data Analysis 21
- 2.6 Comprehension Questions 21
- 2.A Radius of Curvature 21

3 Surface Tension — 24
- 3.1 Introduction — 24
- 3.2 Objective — 24
- 3.3 Theory — 24
  - 3.3.1 Cohesion, Adhesion and Surface Tension — 24
  - 3.3.2 Principles of the Ring Method — 26
- 3.4 Apparatus — 27
- 3.5 Procedure — 28
- 3.6 Comprehension Questions — 30
- 3.A Surface Tension in Soap Film — 30

4 Specific Heat of Solid — 32
- 4.1 Introduction — 32
- 4.2 Objective — 32
- 4.3 Theory — 32
  - 4.3.1 Heat Capacity and Specific Heat — 32
  - 4.3.2 Specific Heat Measurement by Method of Mixture — 33
- 4.4 Apparatus — 33
- 4.5 Procedure — 34
  - 4.5.1 Measurement — 34
  - 4.5.2 Analysis — 36
- 4.6 Comprehension Questions — 37
- 4.A Dulong-Petit Law — 37
- 4.B Newton's Law of Cooling — 39

5 Specific Heat Ratio of Air — 43
- 5.1 Introduction — 43
- 5.2 Objective — 43
- 5.3 Theory — 44
  - 5.3.1 The First Law of Thermodynamics and Specific Heats — 44
  - 5.3.2 Adiabatic Process of Ideal Gas — 45
  - 5.3.3 Equipartition Theorem and Adiabatic Constant — 45
  - 5.3.4 Clément-Désormes Method — 46
- 5.4 Apparatus — 48
  - 5.4.1 Gas Container — 48
  - 5.4.2 Differential Pressure Gauge — 48
  - 5.4.3 Thermistor — 48
- 5.5 Procedure — 49
- 5.6 Comprehension Questions — 50
- 5.A Evaluation of the Temperature Change of Air — 50

6 Diffraction and Interference of Light — 54
- 6.1 Introduction — 54
- 6.2 Objective — 54
- 6.3 Theory — 55
  - 6.3.1 Huygens Principle and Fraunhofer Diffraction — 55
  - 6.3.2 Single-Slit Diffraction — 56

		6.3.3 Diffraction by a Multiple Slit	58
	6.4	Apparatus	60
	6.5	Procedure	61
		6.5.1 Diffraction Due to a Single Slit	61
		6.5.2 Diffraction from Multiple Slits	62
		6.5.3 Two Dimensional Diffraction Grating	63
		6.5.4 Diffraction by Hair	63
	6.6	Comprehension Questions	64
	6.A	Summation of Trigonometric Functions	64

7 Electrical Resistance — 66

- 7.1 Introduction . . . 66
- 7.2 Objective . . . 66
- 7.3 Theory . . . 66
  - 7.3.1 Electrical Resistance of Metals . . . 67
  - 7.3.2 Electrical Resistance of Semiconductors . . . 69
  - 7.3.3 Wheatstone Bridge . . . 70
- 7.4 Apparatus . . . 71
  - 7.4.1 Resistance Box . . . 71
  - 7.4.2 Variable Resistor . . . 71
  - 7.4.3 Galvanometer and Battery . . . 72
  - 7.4.4 Heating Device . . . 72
  - 7.4.5 Sample Resistors . . . 73
- 7.5 Procedure . . . 73
  - 7.5.1 Resistance of Copper Resistor . . . 73
  - 7.5.2 Resistance of Thermistor . . . 74
  - 7.5.3 Data Analysis - Copper Resistor . . . 74
  - 7.5.4 Data Analysis - Thermistor . . . 74
- 7.6 Comprehension Questions . . . 76

8 Thermoelectricity — 78

- 8.1 Introduction . . . 78
- 8.2 Objective . . . 78
- 8.3 Theory . . . 78
  - 8.3.1 The Seebeck Effect . . . 78
  - 8.3.2 The Peltier Effect and the Thomson effect . . . 81
- 8.4 Apparatus . . . 82
  - 8.4.1 Thermocouple . . . 82
  - 8.4.2 Heaters and Heat Baths . . . 82
- 8.5 Procedure . . . 84
  - 8.5.1 Preparation of Cold Junction . . . 84
  - 8.5.2 Setup of Data Acquisition System . . . 84
  - 8.5.3 Measurement of Thermal EMF at the Melting Point of a Metal . . . 85
  - 8.5.4 Thermal EMF at the Boiling Point of Water . . . 86
  - 8.5.5 Thermal EMF at the Boiling Point of Liquid Nitrogen . . . 86
  - 8.5.6 Data Analysis . . . 86

	8.6	Comprehension Questions	86
	8.A	Microscopic View of Thermoelectricity	87

9 Equipotential Lines — 90

- 9.1 Introduction — 90
- 9.2 Objective — 90
- 9.3 Theory — 91
  - 9.3.1 Electric Field and Potential — 91
  - 9.3.2 Potential Due to Lines of Charges — 92
  - 9.3.3 Electrostatic Field and Steady Current Field — 93
- 9.4 Apparatus — 95
- 9.5 Procedure — 95
  - 9.5.1 Setup — 95
  - 9.5.2 Measurement of Equipotentials — 96
  - 9.5.3 Evaluation of Potential Functions — 97
  - 9.5.4 Analysis — 97
- 9.6 Comprehension Questions — 97
- 9.A Derivation of Electric Field Lines — 98

10 AC Circuits and Resonance — 99

- 10.1 Introduction — 99
- 10.2 Objective — 99
- 10.3 Theory — 100
  - 10.3.1 Resistor, Capacitor and Inductor — 100
  - 10.3.2 Series RLC Circuit — 103
  - 10.3.3 Complex Impedance — 104
  - 10.3.4 Resonance in Series RLC Circuit — 108
  - 10.3.5 Resonance in Parallel LC Circuit — 110
- 10.4 Apparatus — 111
  - 10.4.1 ELVIS — 111
  - 10.4.2 RLC Circuit — 111
- 10.5 Procedure — 112
  - 10.5.1 Setup — 112
  - 10.5.2 Phases of V_R, V_L and V_C — 114
  - 10.5.3 Resonance Curve for Series RLC Circuit — 115
  - 10.5.4 Frequency Dependencies of V_L and V_C — 116
  - 10.5.5 Resonance Curve for Parallel LC Circuit — 116
- 10.6 Comprehension Questions — 117

11 Frequency Dependence of Amplifier — 118

- 11.1 Introduction — 118
- 11.2 Objective — 118
- 11.3 Theory — 119
  - 11.3.1 Amplification of RC-Coupled Amplifier — 119
  - 11.3.2 Principles of Oscilloscope — 122
- 11.4 Apparatus — 125
  - 11.4.1 Signal Generator — 125

	11.4.2 Amplifier	126
	11.4.3 Oscilloscope	126
11.5	Procedure	130
	11.5.1 Setup	130
	11.5.2 Measurement of Frequency Dependence of Gain	132
	11.5.3 Data Analysis	133
11.6	Comprehension Questions	134
11.A	Diodes and Transistors	134

12 Absorption of β-Radiation   140

12.1	Introduction	140
12.2	Objective	140
12.3	Theory	141
	12.3.1 Radioactive Decay	141
	12.3.2 β-Radiation	141
	12.3.3 β-Radiations from ^{90}Sr	142
	12.3.4 G-M Tube	143
	12.3.5 Absorption of β-Radiation by Matter	144
12.4	Apparatus	146
12.5	Procedure	146
	12.5.1 Functional Check of Radiation Counter	146
	12.5.2 Determination of Operating Voltage	147
	12.5.3 Background Radiation	148
	12.5.4 Absorption of β-Radiation by Al Plates	148
	12.5.5 Data Analysis	149
12.6	Comprehension Questions	149
12.A	Correction for Counting Loss	150

Index   **151**

Chapter 1

Angular Momentum

1.1 Introduction

Angular momentum is a vector quantity used to describe the rotational motion of solid bodies, and along with energy and linear momentum, it is one of the fundamental quantities that obeys a conservation law. If an external torque is exerted on a body, its angular momentum varies according to the Newton's second law for rotational motions. This laboratory is designed to help you develop an intuitive sense of angular momentum, torque and their relationship through hands-on experience.

1.2 Objective

In this lab, we will

1. confirm the conservation law of angular momentum using a rotating stool, and

2. observe the change in the angular momentum of a gyroscope to verify the equation of motion for a rotating rigid body.

Since the main goal of this experiment is to give you an insight into rotational dynamics and its related quantities, precise measurements and data analysis are not required.

1.3 Theory

We often express physical principles in mechanics using vectors, because vector expressions not only simplify mathematical formulas, but also help us grasp the physical meanings of equations visually. Here we consider the rotational motion of a rigid body; it is a very good example to see the advantages of such vector expressions and you will notice that without vectors, understanding rotational dynamics is quite formidable.

A rigid body is an idealized concept of a solid object which does not undergo any types of deformations. In general, an extended object acted upon by an external force experiences the change in its shape and size as well as the change in its motion. However, it is reasonable to ignore the effect of deformations when the deformations are relatively minor, and we often treat an object as a rigid body to simplify situations.

By definition, interparticle distances are constrained to remain constant in a rigid body. Therefore, if we choose a reference point in a rigid body, the positions of all the other points in the body are fixed with respect to the reference, and we can express the motion of the whole body as the sum of the translational motion of the reference point and the rotational motion about the point. If the mass of a rigid body and the net external force exerted on its center of gravity are both known, it is convenient to take the reference point at the center of gravity, and we can describe the translational motion of the center of gravity exactly in the same way as we do for a point particle. In the following sections we will quickly review the translational motion of a particle and then focus on the pure rotational motion of a rigid body. Note that the complete description of the motion of a rigid body requires three extra coordinates than that of a particle, and these additional degrees of freedom stem from the fact that the rigid bodies are extended, having definite sizes and shapes.

1.3.1 Equation of Translational Motion

First, recall that the equation of motion for a point particle relates the force exerted on the particle to the change in its momentum. The translational motion of a rigid body is expressed exactly in the same way:

$$M\frac{d\boldsymbol{V}}{dt} = \frac{d\boldsymbol{P}}{dt} = \boldsymbol{F}, \tag{1.1}$$

where M, $\boldsymbol{V}$, $\boldsymbol{F}$ are the mass of the rigid body, its velocity and the force exerted at the center of gravity of the body, respectively.

The rotational motion of a rigid body is described as the relationship between the moment of force[1] (**torque**) acted on the body and the rate of change in its moment of momentum (**angular momentum**). We shall now examine the change in the angular momentum of a rigid body acted upon by an external torque.

1.3.2 Torque

A torque is the rotational analogue of a force. As a force causes the change in the translational motion of a particle, a torque causes the change in the rotational motion of an extended object. If a rigid body is free to rotate about a fixed point and a force $\boldsymbol{F}$ is exerted upon it, the effect of the force on the rotation depends not only on the magnitude of the force, but also on its direction and its point of application $\boldsymbol{r}$ with respect to the fixed point. Figure 1.1 (a) shows a rod free to rotate about an

---

[1] In general, for vector $\boldsymbol{A}$ located at position $\boldsymbol{r}$ with respect to the origin, the moment of $\boldsymbol{A}$ about the origin is defined as cross product $\boldsymbol{r} \times \boldsymbol{A}$.

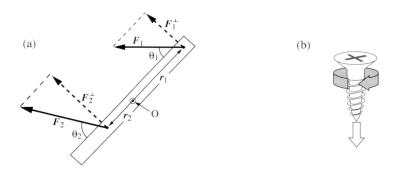

Figure 1.1: (a) Two forces $\boldsymbol{F}_1$ and $\boldsymbol{F}_2$ are exerted on a rod pivoted at point O at positions $\boldsymbol{r}_1$ and $\boldsymbol{r}_2$ respectively. (b) Right-handed screw rule: The direction of torque $\boldsymbol{N}$ due to force $\boldsymbol{F}$ coincides with the direction a right-handed screw advances as the screw is turned by $\boldsymbol{F}^\perp$.

axis through O perpendicular to the page and two forces $\boldsymbol{F}_1$ and $\boldsymbol{F}_2$ acted upon the rod at positions $\boldsymbol{r}_1$ and $\boldsymbol{r}_2$. Since the rod is fixed, the components of the external forces parallel to $\boldsymbol{r}$ are canceled by the constraint force at the pivot point, and only the components perpendicular to $\boldsymbol{r}$ contribute the change in the rotational motion. The perpendicular components of $\boldsymbol{F}_1$ and $\boldsymbol{F}_2$ with respect to $\boldsymbol{r}_1$ and $\boldsymbol{r}_2$ are given by

$$\boldsymbol{F}_1^\perp = \boldsymbol{F}_1 \sin\theta_1, \quad \boldsymbol{F}_2^\perp = \boldsymbol{F}_2 \sin\theta_2, \tag{1.2}$$

where θ_1 and θ_2 be the angles of forces $\boldsymbol{F}_1$ and $\boldsymbol{F}_2$ with respect to the rod. It is experimentally shown that the sizes of $|\boldsymbol{r}||\boldsymbol{F}_\perp| = rF\sin\theta$ determine the direction of the rotation of the rod;[2)] the rod rotates in the clockwise direction if $|\boldsymbol{r}_1||\boldsymbol{F}_1^\perp| < |\boldsymbol{r}_2||\boldsymbol{F}_2^\perp|$ and vice versa. Based on this experimental fact, it is natural to define the magnitude of torque N as

$$N = |\boldsymbol{r}||\boldsymbol{F}^\perp| = rF\sin\theta. \tag{1.3}$$

Although we can indicate the direction of rotation caused by a torque with plus and minus signs for simple situations like Figure 1.1 (a), it is more convenient to define torque as a vector that aligns with the axis of rotation for more general situations. Since $rF\sin\theta$ is equal to the magnitude of the cross product of $\boldsymbol{r}$ and $\boldsymbol{F}$, we define torque as a vector:

$$\boldsymbol{N} = \boldsymbol{r} \times \boldsymbol{F}. \tag{1.4}$$

In Figure 1.1 (a), $\boldsymbol{r}_1 \times \boldsymbol{F}_1$ is directed out of the page and $\boldsymbol{r}_2 \times \boldsymbol{F}_2$ is into the page. The direction of $\boldsymbol{N}$ due to a force is determined by the direction a right-handed screw advances when the screw is rotated by $\boldsymbol{F}^\perp$ as shown in Figure 1.1 (b)

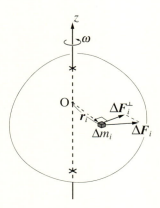

Figure 1.2: $\Delta \boldsymbol{F}_i$ is acted upon mass element Δm_i located at $\boldsymbol{r}_i$ with respect to O.

1.3.3 Angular Momentum

Next we consider the effect of torques on the rotational motion of a rigid body. For this purpose, we regard a rigid body as a collection of small mass elements and focus on the motion of one of these elements first. We can find the net effect of external torques on the whole rigid body as the sum of the effects on its mass elements later. Figure 1.2 shows the ith mass element $\Delta \boldsymbol{m}_i$ at position $\boldsymbol{r}_i$ with respect to O rotating around an axis passing through O and force $\Delta \boldsymbol{F}_i$ exerted on the element. Because the motion of the element is confined in a circular path, the acceleration along the path is determined by the component of force $\Delta \boldsymbol{F}_i$ tangent to the circle. The Newton's second law in the tangential direction yields

$$\Delta \boldsymbol{F}_i^{\perp} = \Delta m_i \frac{\mathrm{d}\boldsymbol{v}_i}{\mathrm{d}t} = \frac{\mathrm{d}}{\mathrm{d}t}\Delta \boldsymbol{P}_i, \tag{1.5}$$

where $\boldsymbol{v}_i$ and $\Delta \boldsymbol{P}_i$ are the velocity and the momentum of the element respectively. Taking the cross product of the equation with position vector $\boldsymbol{r}_i$ and rewriting it using torque $\Delta \boldsymbol{N}_i$, we obtain

$$\Delta \boldsymbol{N}_i = \boldsymbol{r}_i \times \Delta \boldsymbol{F}_i = \boldsymbol{r}_i \times \frac{\mathrm{d}}{\mathrm{d}t}\Delta \boldsymbol{P}_i = \frac{\mathrm{d}}{\mathrm{d}t}\Delta \boldsymbol{L}_i. \tag{1.6}$$

In the last expression we defined angular momentum $\Delta \boldsymbol{L}_i$ of mass element $\Delta \boldsymbol{m}_i$ as the moment (cross product) of linear momentum $\Delta \boldsymbol{P}_i$:

$$\Delta \boldsymbol{L}_i = \boldsymbol{r}_i \times \Delta \boldsymbol{P}_i, \tag{1.7}$$

and used the fact that the derivative of $\boldsymbol{r}_i$ is parallel to the momentum and their vector product vanishes:

$$\frac{\mathrm{d}}{\mathrm{d}t}\Delta \boldsymbol{L}_i = \dot{\boldsymbol{r}}_i \times \Delta \boldsymbol{P}_i + \boldsymbol{r}_i \times \frac{\mathrm{d}}{\mathrm{d}t}\Delta \boldsymbol{P}_i = \boldsymbol{r}_i \times \frac{\mathrm{d}}{\mathrm{d}t}\Delta \boldsymbol{P}_i. \tag{1.8}$$

---

[2] $r \sin \theta$ represents the perpendicular distance between the rotational axis and the line of action of the force, and is called the *moment arm* or *lever arm* of $\boldsymbol{F}$.

1.3 THEORY

To find out the response of a rigid body to a net torque, we sum up Equation (1.6) over the whole body. The result is

$$\boldsymbol{N} = \sum_i \Delta \boldsymbol{N}_i = \sum_i \frac{\mathrm{d}}{\mathrm{d}t} \Delta \boldsymbol{L}_i = \frac{\mathrm{d}}{\mathrm{d}t} \boldsymbol{L}, \tag{1.9}$$

where $\boldsymbol{N}$ is the net external torque exerted on the whole rigid body and $\boldsymbol{L}$ is the total angular momentum of the body. Equation (1.9) states that *the rate of change in the angular momentum of a rigid body is equal to the net external torque acted on the body*. Although here we have derived the equation for a rigid body fixed on an axis, it holds true for any system of particles as well as freely moving rigid bodies, and is considered one of the fundamental equations of mechanics.

1.3.4 Moment of Inertia and the Newton's 2nd Law for Rotation

For a rigid body free to rotate about a fixed axis, it is advantageous to introduce angular velocity vector $\boldsymbol{\omega}$ that has the magnitude of $\omega = \mathrm{d}\theta/\mathrm{d}t$ [rad/s] and is along the rotational axis in the direction specified by the right-handed screw rule (Figure 1.1 (b)). Then velocity $\boldsymbol{v}$ of any element of a rotating rigid body at position $\boldsymbol{r}$ with respect to O on its rotational axis is expressed in terms of this single common variable $\boldsymbol{\omega}$:

$$\boldsymbol{v} = \boldsymbol{\omega} \times \boldsymbol{r}. \tag{1.10}$$

Rewriting Equation (1.9) using the angular velocity vector, we obtain

$$\sum_i \boldsymbol{r}_i \times \frac{\mathrm{d}}{\mathrm{d}t} \Delta \boldsymbol{P}_i = \sum_i \Delta m_i \frac{\mathrm{d}}{\mathrm{d}t} (\boldsymbol{r}_i \times (\boldsymbol{\omega} \times \boldsymbol{r}_i))$$

$$= \sum_i \Delta m_i \frac{\mathrm{d}}{\mathrm{d}t} (\boldsymbol{\omega}(\boldsymbol{r}_i)^2 - \boldsymbol{r}_i(\boldsymbol{\omega} \cdot \boldsymbol{r}_i)). \tag{1.11}$$

Here we used an identity for the vector triple product.[3] To reduce the equation further, we take the rotational axis of a spinning body along the z-axis as in Figure 1.2 and assume that the body is limited in the plane containing O and perpendicular to the z-axis. Then $\boldsymbol{\omega}$ has the z-component only and $\boldsymbol{r}_i$ has the x- and y-components only. Equation (1.11) yields

$$\sum_i \boldsymbol{r}_i \times \frac{\mathrm{d}}{\mathrm{d}t} \Delta \boldsymbol{P}_i = \sum_i \Delta m_i \frac{\mathrm{d}}{\mathrm{d}t} \omega_z (x_i^2 + y_i^2) \boldsymbol{e}_z$$

$$= \sum_i \Delta m_i r_i^2 \frac{\mathrm{d}}{\mathrm{d}t} \omega_z \boldsymbol{e}_z. \tag{1.12}$$

Introducing a new symbol

$$I = \sum_i \Delta m_i r_i^2 \tag{1.13}$$

---

[3] For three vectors $\boldsymbol{A}$, $\boldsymbol{B}$ and $\boldsymbol{C}$, the vector triple product is defined as $\boldsymbol{A} \times (\boldsymbol{B} \times \boldsymbol{C})$. Refer to a textbook on vector analysis for its expansion formula.

and rewriting Equation (1.9) using I, we obtain the Newton's second law in angular form:

$$I\frac{d\boldsymbol{\omega}}{dt} = \frac{d\boldsymbol{L}}{dt} = \boldsymbol{N}. \tag{1.14}$$

Scalar quantity I is called the **moment of inertia** (a.k.a. rotational inertia) about a z-axis, and is an intrinsic quantity of a rigid body which only depends on the geometry of the body and not on its state of motion. Keep in mind that the moment of inertia still depends on your choice of a rotational axis. Also, you should remark that we have derived Equation (1.14) for a plane figure, and angular momentum $\boldsymbol{L}$ is *not* always in parallel with angular velocity $\boldsymbol{\omega}$ for bodies of arbitrary three dimensional shapes.[4] However, if the rotational axis of a symmetrical object coincides with its line of symmetry, as in the case of the experiments we are performing in this laboratory, the angular momentum aligns with the angular velocity.[5] Therefore, you can safely assume that the angular velocity and angular momentum are both directed along the axis of rotation in this experiment.

Equation (1.14) makes analogy between translational motions and rotational motions clear; as the mass of a particle serves as resistance to a force, the moment of inertia of a rigid body serves as resistance to a torque, and the product of the moment of inertia and the angular velocity defines the angular momentum ($\boldsymbol{L} = I\boldsymbol{\omega}$) the same way as the product of the mass and the velocity defines linear momentum ($\boldsymbol{P} = m\boldsymbol{v}$). The table below summarizes the correspondence between the linear quantities and the rotational quantities:

Type of motion	Translational motion	Rotational motion
Inertial property	Mass M	Moment of inertia I
Time-dependent coordinates	Position (x, y, z)	Angle θ
Rate of change in coordinates	Velocity $\boldsymbol{V}$	Angular velocity $\boldsymbol{\omega}$
State of motion	Momentum $\boldsymbol{P}$	Angular momentum $\boldsymbol{L}$
Influence on motion	Force $\boldsymbol{F}$	Torque $\boldsymbol{N}$

1.3.5 Parallel-Axis Theorem

In principle, we can calculate the moment of inertia of any extended objects using Equation (1.13). However, if a rigid body does not have any symmetry about an axis in consideration, the direct calculation of the moment of inertia about the axis often becomes complicated. Fortunately, we have a convenient theorem, known as the parallel-axis theorem, to avoid such complicated calculations if we already know the moment of inertia about an axis passing through the center of gravity[6] (known as a centroidal axis), and if the centroidal axis is parallel to a new axis about which

---

[4] In general, the angular momentum of a rigid body is given by $\boldsymbol{L} = [I]\boldsymbol{\omega}$, where $[I]$ is a three by three matrix called the moment of inertia tensor. The directions of $\boldsymbol{L}$ and $\boldsymbol{\omega}$ do not match unless the off-diagonal elements of $[I]$ vanish.

[5] It is known that for any rigid body, there are a set of three orthogonal axes around which the directions of $\boldsymbol{\omega}$ and $\boldsymbol{L}$ agree. Such rotational axes are called the *principal axes*.

[6] The moments of inertia of simple symmetrical objects about axes along their lines of symmetry are found in almost any mechanics textbooks.

1.4 APPARATUS

Figure 1.3: Bicycle Wheel Experiment. A bicycle wheel is spun while being held vertically (left) and then tilted (right).

we wish to calculate the moment of inertia. According to the theorem, the moment of inertia about the new axis is

$$I = I_G + Mh^2, \tag{1.15}$$

where I_G is the moment of inertia about the centroidal axis, M is the total mass of the rigid body, and h is the distance between the two parallel axes. This theorem also implies that the moment of inertia about an axis passing through the center of gravity is always the smallest among the set of moments of inertia about various parallel axes.

1.4 Apparatus

1. Rotating stool and bicycle wheel with handles.
2. Rotating stool, pair of dumbbells, tape measure and stopwatch.
3. Gyroscope, weights and stop watch.

1.5 Procedure

1.5.1 Spinning Bicycle Wheel

In this part of the lab we observe what happens when we tilt a spinning wheel while sitting on a rotating stool as shown in Figure 1.3. Before conducting the experiment, sketch the stool, the person on the stool and the wheel, and answer the following questions to make a prediction on the outcome of tilting the wheel.

Figure 1.4: Dumbbell Experiment. A pair of dumbbells are held at the sides of one's body while the stool is rotating (left), then the arms are outstretched (right).

- How does the direction of the angular momentum of the wheel change before and after tilting the wheel? Draw angular momentum $\boldsymbol{L}$ before and after tilting in the sketch.

- Draw torque $\boldsymbol{N}$ exerted on the wheel by the person. If you regard the stool, the person on the stool and the wheel as a system, are there external forces exerted on the system when the wheel is tilted?

- Refer to Equation (1.14). How does the angular momentum of the system change before and after tilting the wheel?

Now let's try it out. Sit on the stool on the rotating platform so that your center of gravity is directly above the spinning axis of the stool. Hold the bicycle wheel at the handles and have your partner spin the wheel in the vertical plane passing through the axis of the stool. Get your feet off the floor and then turn the wheel to the left or to the right. Record the direction of the spin of the wheel and the direction of the tilt in your notebook. Take turns with your partner and repeat the experiment several times with different directions of spinning and tilting. Compare the result with your prediction.

1.5.2 Rotating Stool and Dumbbells

Have a seat on the stool with a dumbbell in each hand. Rotate the stool while keeping your arms close to your body, and then outstretch your arms as shown in Figure 1.4,[7] and observe how the rotational speed of the stool varies as you stretch or tuck your arms. Take turns with your partner. Does this change in the angular speed agree with what you expect from Equation (1.14)? To examine the

---

[7] Caution: If you spin the stool with your arms extended and then tuck your arms in, you might spin too fast and shoot yourself from the stool. Please be careful.

1.5 PROCEDURE

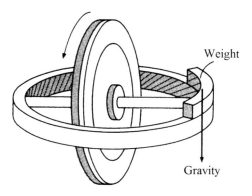

Figure 1.5: Gyroscope experiment. A weight is put on the inner gimbal of a gyroscope while its rotor is spinning.

relationship between the angular velocity and the moment of inertia more closely, measure rotational periods with a stopwatch both while your arms at the side of your body T_1 and extended away from your body T_2. You need to finish the two measurements in a row without stopping the stool. To get more accurate results, do not measure the periods directly. Rather, measure a time interval for several rotations and then divide it by the number of rotations. Calculate the angular speeds for both of the situations (ω_1 and ω_2). Also, using a tape measure, measure the rotational radii of the dumbbells both as your arms tucked r_1 and extended r_2. Compute the moments of inertia of the dumbbells for both cases (I_1 and I_2). Answer Comprehension Question 1.

1.5.3 Gyroscope

In this part of the experiment we will examine the angular momentum of a gyroscope to check the equation of motion for rotations expressed as Equation (1.14). The gyroscope used in this lab consists of a rotor (a massive spinning disk) supported by two gimbals (pivoted rings) free to rotate about axes perpendicular to each other. The gimbals are mounted on an outer frame whose orientation can also be adjusted at a joint on the bottom of the frame. With the two gimbals and the adjustable frame, the rotor can spin in any orientation. Because the bearings at the ends of the rotor axis are quite delicate to allow smooth rotation of the rotor, please be careful not to handle it roughly.

We will use an electric drill to spin the rotor. The electric drill equipped on your table has a disk covered with a rubber ring attached to it. To spin the gyroscope, bring the edge of the disk into contact with the edge of the rotor and pull the trigger of the drill. The trigger is pressure sensitive so that you can adjust the spinning speed of the disk as necessary. First pull the trigger gently and then squeeze harder for faster rotation. To achieve the maximum speed of the rotor, put the disk in contact with the axis of the rotor.

1. Since the center of gravity of the rotor is on its rotational axis, the torque to due the gravity about the axis is zero. Therefore, if there is no other external torques exerted on the rotor, the angular momentum of the rotor is conserved. This means that the rotor's plane of rotation is preserved even when you change the orientation of the gyroscope. Check this by actually varying the orientation of the frame. Spin the gyroscope to the maximum speed, hold the outer frame, and then loosen the wing nut at the bottom of the frame to tilt the gyroscope. While the gyroscope is tilted, rotate it around a vertical axis using the handle located near the wing nut. If the gyroscope is too rigid to be moved around, loosen the bolt on the opposite side of the handle.

2. Next we will observe the motion of the gyroscope while a weight is placed on the inner gimbal as shown in Figure 1.5. Before conducting the experiment, sketch a top view of the gyroscope (the rotor and the inner gimbal only) so that you can record the direction of the spin of the rotor, the position of the weight placed on the gimbal, and the change in the direction of the rotational axis of the rotor. The change in the rotational axis of a gyroscope is called *precession*. Spin the gyroscope and direct its axis horizontal. Then put a weight on the inner gimbal and record the motion of the gyroscope.

   Did the gyroscope move as you expected? To explain the precession of the gyroscope, refer to Equation (1.14). Treating the time derivative of angular momentum as the change in angular momentum $\Delta \boldsymbol{L}$ during small time interval Δt, we have

   $$\Delta \boldsymbol{L} = \boldsymbol{N} \Delta t. \qquad (1.16)$$

   This equation tells you that the change in the angular momentum of the gyroscope points in the same direction as the torque due to the gravitational force on the weight. Draw the angular momentum vector of the spinning rotor and the torque vector due to the gravity on the weight in your sketch, and check if the direction of the gyroscope's precession agrees with the direction predicted from Equation (1.16).

3. Equation (1.16) not only tells you the direction of the precession, but also its precession rate (the angular speed of the rotation of the rotor axis). Here we alter two quantities, the spinning speed of the rotor and the weight placed on the gimbal, and analyze their influence on the precession rate of the gyroscope. First, put a weight on the gimbal while the rotor is spinning in the vertical plane, tap the edge of the rotor lightly to slow it down, and watch the change in the precession rate. Did the precession get faster or slower? Record the result. Second, measure the periods the precession while one weight (m) is on the gimbal and while two weights ($2m$) are stacked. You need to conduct these two measurements consecutively so as not to let the spinning speed of the rotor change, for the rotor is always slowing down due to friction at the bearings. Therefore, you will get more accurate results if you measure the time intervals for a half or a quarter of a precession and calculate the periods

rather than measure the periods directly. Compute the precession rates, and answer Comprehension Question 2.

1.6 Comprehension Questions

1. Estimate the moment of inertia of the system consisting of the stool and a person on the stool I_0. Because no external force is exerted on the whole system consisting of the stool, the person and the dumbbells while extending your arms, the total angular momentum of the system is conserved. Ignoring the change in the moment of inertia of the arms for simplicity, equation (1.14) yields

$$(I_0 + I_1)\omega_1 = (I_0 + I_2)\omega_2. \tag{1.17}$$

Solve the equation for I_0 and evaluate the total moment of inertia of a person and a stool.

2. Discuss the dependency of the precession rate of the gyroscope on the spinning speed of the rotor and the amount of the weight placed on the gimbal. If the precession rate of the gyroscope is Ω, the small change in the angle of the axis of the rotor during time interval Δt is given by $\Omega \Delta t$. Combine this with Equation (1.16) and express precession rate Ω in terms of mass m on the gimbal and spinning speed ω of the rotor.

Chapter 2

Young's Modulus

2.1 Introduction

A stationary solid body acted upon by a force deforms. However, if the force is relatively small, in many cases the deformation is not permanent and the body restores its original size and shape once the force is removed. This property of solid bodies is called *elasticity*. The relationship between a deforming force on a body and the change in its dimensions is described in terms of *stress*, force per unit area, and *strain*, fractional change in its dimensions. Stress and strain are proportional to each other over a wide range of practical usefulness, and their proportionality constant is called the *modulus of elasticity*. Therefore, the general relation between stress and strain is expressed as

$$\text{stress} = \text{modulus} \times \text{strain}. \qquad (2.1)$$

There are several different types of elastic moduli, but they are not always all independent. For example, it is known that the elastic property of a homogenous isotropic material is uniquely determined by two elastic moduli only, and other moduli can be described in terms of the two. In this experiment, we will learn that two different types of deformations can actually be represented by only one elastic modulus.

2.2 Objective

We will determine the Young's moduli of metal beams by means of flexure. The small deflections of the beams will be magnified and measured precisely by a mechanism called the optical lever. Familiarizing ourselves with the principles of the optical lever also makes an important part of this experiment because it has a wide range of application in physics and engineering.

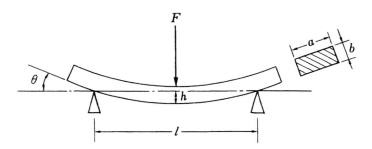

Figure 2.1: Deflection of a beam acted upon by force $\boldsymbol{F}$ at the center of two supports.

2.3 Theory

2.3.1 Young's Modulus

When equal and opposite normal forces are exerted on the opposite sides of a solid bar, it is simply compressed or stretched. The tensile or compressive stress is defined by T/S, where T is the magnitude of the normal force and S is the cross sectional area of the bar. The strain is $\Delta L/L$, the fractional change in the length of the bar. The proportionality constants for tension and compression are almost the same for many materials within their elastic limits,[1] and the modulus is called the **Young's modulus**. By definition, Young's modulus E is given by

$$E = \frac{\text{stress}}{\text{strain}} = \frac{\frac{T}{S}}{\frac{\Delta l}{l}}. \qquad (2.2)$$

The Young's modulus only depends on the types of materials and not on the geometry of a specimen, and is a measure of the stiffness of a material; a stiffer material has a greater value of the Young's modulus than a softer material.

2.3.2 Flexure of a Beam and Young's Modulus

The simplest way to determine the Young's modulus of a material is to measure the elongation of a material sample under a tension. However, it can be determined by giving the material a different type of deformation. Figure 2.1 illustrates a beam with rectangular cross section of width a and height b placed on two knife-edge supports separated by distance l; force $\boldsymbol{F}$ is exerted on the beam at the midpoint between the two supports, and the beam sags by amount h and each end of the beam makes angle θ to the horizontal. As we shall see in the following argument, the Young's modulus can be determined by measuring h or θ.

---

[1] The elastic limits themselves are often very different for the two types of stress. Concrete, for instance, is strong in compression but very weak in tension.

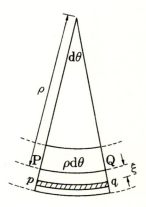
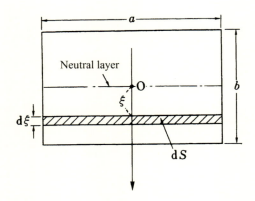

Figure 2.2: A small element in the beam bounded by two neighboring points P and Q.

Figure 2.3: A transverse cross section inside the element shown in Figure 2.2. The cross sectional area of differential layer pq is $\mathrm{d}S = a\,\mathrm{d}\xi$.

As the beam flexes as in Figure 2.1, the upper surface of the beam is compressed and the lower surface is stretched.[2] Therefore, there must be an intermediate layer, called the *neutral layer*, which does not undergo any change in length. The stress in the neutral layer is zero, and the stress and strain get larger in layers farther from the neutral layer. To examine the relationship between stress and strain in longitudinal layers inside the beam, we focus on the small element of the beam dissected by the two cross sections containing nearby points P and Q as shown in Figure 2.2. The arc PQ represents a part of the neutral layer, and the arc pq is a layer below the neutral layer by distance ξ. Denoting the radius of curvature of the element by ρ, the length of the neutral layer in the element is $\rho\,\mathrm{d}\theta$, and the length of layer pq is $(\rho + \xi)\,\mathrm{d}\theta$. The tensile strain of the layer pq is

$$\frac{(\rho+\xi)\mathrm{d}\theta - \rho\,\mathrm{d}\theta}{\rho\,\mathrm{d}\theta} = \frac{\xi}{\rho}. \tag{2.3}$$

Since stress is proportional to strain, tensile or compressive force $\mathrm{d}T$ on the cross section $\mathrm{d}S$ of layer pq (Figure 2.3) is expresses as

$$\mathrm{d}T = \frac{E\xi}{\rho}\mathrm{d}S. \tag{2.4}$$

Note that the force is tensile for $\xi > 0$ and compressive for $\xi < 0$. Due to the symmetry of the beam, the neutral layer agrees with the central layer of the beam

---

[2] Flexure actually involves both tensile strain and shear strain (deformation due to a force parallel to a cross section). However, if the deflection is small, the effect of shear is negligible and we can treat the deformation simply as compression and extension.

and the net force on the cross section of the whole element vanishes:

$$T = \int \frac{E\xi}{\rho} dS = \frac{E}{\rho} \int_{-\frac{b}{2}}^{\frac{b}{2}} \xi a d\xi = 0. \tag{2.5}$$

Nonetheless, the moment of the force with respect to the neutral layer (**bending moment**) on the whole cross section does not disappear:

$$N = \int \xi dT = \frac{E}{\rho} \int_{-\frac{b}{2}}^{\frac{b}{2}} \xi^2 a d\xi = \frac{E}{\rho} \frac{ab^3}{12}. \tag{2.6}$$

Note that the bending moment at cross section P is in the clockwise direction, and that at Q is counterclockwise. Equation (2.6) indicates that if we are able to measure bending moment N and radius of curvature ρ, we can obtain the Young's modulus from Equation (2.6).

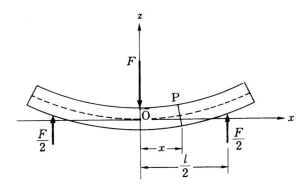

Figure 2.4: Free body diagram of the beam shown in Figure 2.1 with coordinate axes. The origin of the coordinate system is chosen at the geometric center of the beam.

To associate the bending moment N and the radius of curvature ρ with the applied force F and the angle of the ends of the beam with respect to x-axis (θ in Figure 2.1) respectively, we take the origin O of our coordinate system at the center of the beam, z-axis vertically upward and x-axis in the longitudinal direction as described in Figure 2.4. First, we consider the equilibrium condition of the portion of the beam to the right of the cross section P. For this portion to be balanced, the bending moment at the cross section must be canceled by the upward force at the knife-edge support on the right. The equilibrium condition yields

$$N = \left(\frac{l}{2} - x\right) \frac{F}{2}. \tag{2.7}$$

This equation relates the bending moment N with the force F applied to the beam.

Next, let us represent the intersection of the neutral layer and the xz-plane by curve $z = f(x)$. The radius of curvature ρ at an arbitrary point in the curve is given by[3]

$$\rho = \frac{\left\{1 + \left(\frac{\mathrm{d}z}{\mathrm{d}x}\right)^2\right\}^{\frac{3}{2}}}{\frac{\mathrm{d}^2 z}{\mathrm{d}x^2}}. \tag{2.8}$$

If the deflection of the beam is small, then $\frac{\mathrm{d}z}{\mathrm{d}x}$ is negligible compared to 1, and we can drop $\left(\frac{\mathrm{d}z}{\mathrm{d}x}\right)^2$ from the numerator in Equation (2.8). Plugging Equations (2.7) and (2.8) into Equation (2.6), we get

$$\frac{\mathrm{d}^2 z}{\mathrm{d}x^2} = \frac{6F}{Eab^3}\left(\frac{l}{2} - x\right). \tag{2.9}$$

Integrating from 0 to x, the equation becomes

$$\frac{\mathrm{d}z}{\mathrm{d}x} = \frac{6F}{Eab^3}\left(\frac{lx}{2} - \frac{x^2}{2}\right), \tag{2.10}$$

where we used the fact that the slope $\frac{\mathrm{d}z}{\mathrm{d}x}$ is zero at the center ($x = 0$) of the beam. The angle of the beam at the position of the support θ is approximated by

$$\theta \cong \tan\theta = \left.\frac{\mathrm{d}z}{\mathrm{d}x}\right|_{x=\frac{l}{2}} = \frac{3}{4}\frac{Fl^2}{Eab^3}. \tag{2.11}$$

The amount of the flexure h is obtained by integrating Equation (2.10) once more and evaluating the result at one of the supports:

$$h = \left.z\right|_{x=\frac{l}{2}} = \frac{Fl^3}{4Eab^3}. \tag{2.12}$$

2.3.3 Optical Lever

In this experiment, we will measure the angle θ of the beam with respect to the horizontal to find the Young modulus E. Since this angle is minute, we need to magnify its reading to measure it to a reasonable degree of precision and obtain a meaningful result. We will use a device called an *optical lever*, which consists of a set of mirrors attached to an object of interest and a scale placed at a distance from the object.

---

[3] Refer to 2.A Radius of Curvature.

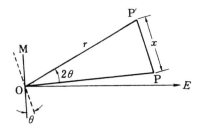 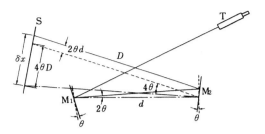

Figure 2.5: Relationship between angular displacement θ and linear displacement x. Mirror M is viewed from E (eye).

Figure 2.6: Change in scale reading δx as two mirrors are tilted by θ. Light rays from scale S are reflected twice at M_2 and M_1 before reaching telescope T.

Figure 2.5 shows the change in scale readings due to a small angular displacement of a mirror. Suppose you look at the mirror M from E and a scale reading P is observed at first. If the mirror is rotated by a slight angle θ, you will see P'. The angle between the incident ray and the reflected ray increases by 2θ, and if θ is small, the linear displacement $x\,(=\overline{PP'})$ is approximated by

$$2r\theta \cong x, \tag{2.13}$$

where $r = \overline{OP} = \overline{OP'}$. Thus we can find θ by measuring r and x.

Figure 2.6 illustrates scale S viewed from telescope T through mirrors M_1 and M_2. Today, mirrors will be mounted near the ends of a beam and they will tilt in the opposite directions by the same amount due to a flexure of the beam (Figure 2.1). If the mirrors tilt by an angle of θ, the direction of the ray after reflected twice from the mirrors varies by 4θ. Denoting the distance between M_1 and M_2 by d and that between M_2 and scale S by D, the change in the scale reading δx, according to Figure 2.6, is written as

$$\delta x = 4\theta D + 2\theta d. \tag{2.14}$$

Substituting this into Equation (2.11) and removing θ, we obtain

$$E = \frac{3(2D+d)l^2}{2ab^3}\frac{F}{\delta x}. \tag{2.15}$$

We will measure a, b, l, d, D, F and δx to determine the Young's modulus E.

2.4 Apparatus

2.4.1 Young's Modulus Apparatus

Figure 2.7 illustrates the Young's modulus apparatus used in this laboratory. A and B are knife-edge supports on which a metal beam will be placed. E is a movable knife-edge positioned at the center of AB from which a weight holder is suspended.

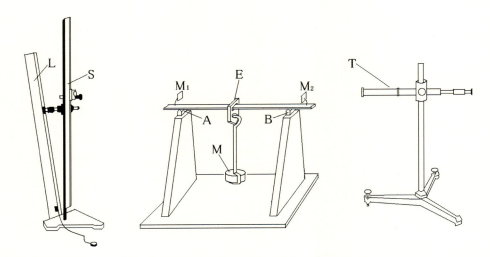

Figure 2.7: Young's modulus apparatus. L: Light. S: Scale. M_1 and M_2: Mirrors. A and B: Knife edge supports. E: Movable knife edge. M: Weight. T: Telescope.

A downward force will be applied by placing weights on the holder to flex the beam. S is a scale with a least count of 1 mm and L is a fluorescent light stand to illuminate the scale. We will adjust the position of telescope T so that light from the scale goes into the telescope after reflected at M_2 and then M_1.

2.4.2 Telescope

The telescope used in this laboratory is depicted in Figure 2.8. It is mounted on vertical stand A with horizontal beam B. We can adjust the height of the telescope by loosening F_1, and F_2 is used to change the angle of the telescope in a vertical plane. S_1 and S_2 are screws for fine adjustment in vertical direction and horizontal direction respectively. O is the objective lens and E is the eyepiece of the telescope. We can alter the position of E with fine adjustment screw S_3 to focus on an object of interest. If the image of the reticle in the eyepiece is blur, turn the rim of the eyepiece S_4 for a sharper image.

2.4.3 Others

We have three metal beams made of different materials: iron, copper and brass. A bending force will be applied with eight 200-g weights. l, d and D will be measured with a tape measure, and we will use a Vernier caliper to measure a and b.

2.5 PROCEDURE

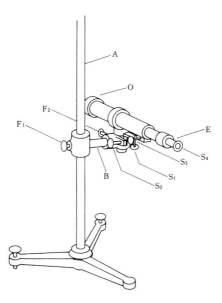

Figure 2.8: Telescope. A and B: Vertical and horizontal supports. F_1 and F_2: Fixation screws for coarse adjustment. S_1–S_4: Fine adjustment screws. O: Objective. E: Eyepiece.

2.5 Procedure

2.5.1 Setup

First we will make several preliminary measurements and assemble the apparatus:

1. Measure distance l between the two knife-edge supports on the Young's modulus apparatus using the tape measure.

2. Measure width a and height b of one of the metal beams using the Vernier caliper. Measure each of the dimensions several times at different locations and calculate an average value for each.

3. Attach the movable knife-edge to the beam and place the beam on the knife-edge supports on the apparatus and hang the weight holder from the movable knife-edge as shown in Figure 2.7. Set it exactly at the midpoint between the two supports.

4. Attach the two mirrors near the ends of the beam so that they face each other, and measure distance d between the two mirrors.

5. Place the scale S vertically in the back of M_1 and adjust the position of the fluorescent light stand as necessary. Although the change in the scale reading

δx is proportional to the distance between M_2 and S, a larger distance between M_2 and S also makes a measurement harder because a small vibration of the beam would make the image of the scale reading unstable. Setting the distance from 0.5 m to 1 m is supposed to be appropriate.

6. Place the telescope T in the back of the mirror M_2 so that S, M_1, M_2 and T are all in a straight line.

2.5.2 Adjustment of Telescope

Next, we will adjust the telescope in order to get a sharp image of the vertical scale produced by the two mirrors:

1. Look at M_2 from a position exactly in front of the scale (or move the scale sideways and look at the scale from the position where the scale was located), and adjust the direction of the mirror M_2 so that the image of the mirror M_1 is seen in M_2. If you have changed the position of the scale, move it back to its original position.

2. Displace the telescope slightly to one side and look at M_1 from the position where the telescope was positioned. Adjust the angle of M_1 so that the image of M_2 with the image of the scale inside M_2 can be seen.

3. Place the telescope back to its original position, and adjust its height and direction to get the image of M_1. It is easier to get the image if you place the telescope about 20 cm away from M_2. The focal length of the telescope is relatively long, so do not expect you would get a sharp image of M_1.

4. Turn the fine adjustment screw S_3 to focus on the scale. To get accurate results, it is preferable to set S, M_1, M_2 and T at almost the same height and in a straight line. However, it may make the measurement harder due to light coming into the telescope directly from the scale. In that case, slightly move the scale to the left or right from the optical axis of the telescope.

5. Measure distance D between M_2 and S. Make sure you have all values of a, b, l, d and D before proceeding to the next step.

2.5.3 Measurement

Record the scale reading at the center of the reticle of in the eyepiece. Readings should be performed to 0.1 mm. Place a 200-g mass on the weight holder and record the reading again. To accurately determine the change in the scale reading, one student should keep viewing the image of the scale while a mass is being placed on the holder by another student, for the position of the reticle depends on the position of the viewer's eye. Add a mass one by one and record the reading up to a total mass of 1,400 g (seven weights).

2.5.4 Data Analysis

1. Rewriting Equation (2.15) in terms of mass m of the weights suspended from the beam, we have

$$E = \frac{3(2D+d)l^2}{2ab^3} \frac{m}{\delta x} g = \frac{3(2D+d)l^2 g}{2ab^3} \frac{1}{(\delta x/m)}, \qquad (2.16)$$

where g is the gravitational acceleration.

2. If you plot a graph of the scale reading x versus the mass of the weights m, the slope of the graph gives a best value of $(\delta x/m)$. Using your measured values of the scale reading, plot a scale reading vs. mass graph on a piece of graph paper and evaluate the slope of the graph.

3. Compute the Young's modulus in SI unit (N/m^2) for each beam using Equation (2.16).

2.6 Comprehension Questions

1. Conduct the integration of Equation (2.10) on your own and confirm the amount of flexure h is actually given by Equation (2.12).

2. Evaluate the maximum amount of h we attained today. Manipulating Equations (2.11), (2.12) and (2.14), first express h in terms of δx and then plug the value of δx you obtained when the maximum amount of load (1,400 g) is applied to the beam.

3. In this laboratory, we did not exert a tensile force on a beam and measure its elongation directly, but subject the beam to a flexural force and determined the Young's modulus indirectly. Which method of the two measurements yields more precise result in general? Roughly estimate an elongation of the beam you would obtain by applying a reasonably strong force feasible in the laboratory, and compare it with the amount of flexure h we achieved in this experiment.

2.A Radius of Curvature

If two points on a curve P and Q are close enough, the section PQ of the curve is approximated by an arc of a circle; as shown in Figure 2.9, let C be the center of the circle, ρ be the radius of the circle and θ be $\angle PCQ$. Arc length Δs between P and Q is given by

$$\Delta s = \rho \Delta \theta. \qquad (2.17)$$

As Q approaches P along the curve, the approximate circle approaches a circle tangent at P, and the circle in this limit is called the *osculating circle* of the curve at point P; the radius and the center of the osculating circle are the **radius of** curvature and the **center of curvature** respectively. The radius of curvature ρ is defined by

$$\rho = \lim_{\Delta\theta \to 0} \frac{\Delta s}{\Delta \theta} = \frac{ds}{d\theta}. \quad (2.18)$$

If we denote the angle of the tangent vector at P with respect to the x-axis by θ, then the angle of the tangent vector at Q is expressed as $\theta + \Delta\theta$ because the tangent vectors are perpendicular to the radii of the approximate circle. The **curvature** of a curve at a point on the curve is defined as the rate of change in the angle of the tangent vector at the point; mathematically, it is

$$\kappa = \lim_{\Delta s \to 0} \frac{\Delta \theta}{\Delta s} = \frac{d\theta}{ds} = \frac{1}{\rho}. \quad (2.19)$$

Therefore, the curvature is the reciprocal of the radius of the osculating circle.

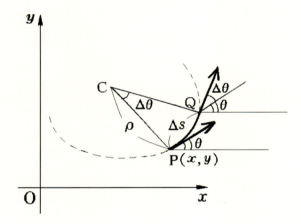

Figure 2.9: Two nearby points P and Q on a curve and center of osculating circle C.

New we shall derive Equation (2.8). Suppose we have a planer curve $y = f(x)$, the slope of a tangent line at an arbitrary point in the curve is given by

$$\frac{dy}{dx} = \tan\theta. \quad (2.20)$$

Thus the angle of the tangent vector with respect to the x-axis is expressed as

$$\theta = \tan^{-1}\frac{dy}{dx}. \quad (2.21)$$

2.A RADIUS OF CURVATURE

Using $(\tan^{-1} x)' = \dfrac{1}{1+x^2}$, we get

$$\frac{d\theta}{dx} = \frac{d}{dx}\left(\tan^{-1}\frac{dy}{dx}\right) = \frac{\left(\dfrac{dy}{dx}\right)'}{1+\left(\dfrac{dy}{dx}\right)^2} = \frac{\dfrac{d^2 y}{dx^2}}{1+\left(\dfrac{dy}{dx}\right)^2}. \tag{2.22}$$

On the other hand, differential arc length ds is given by

$$ds = \sqrt{dx^2 + dy^2}. \tag{2.23}$$

Differentiating with respect to x yields

$$\frac{ds}{dx} = \sqrt{1+\left(\frac{dy}{dx}\right)^2}. \tag{2.24}$$

Using the chain rule and substituting Equations (2.22) and (2.24) into Equation (2.18), we finally find our final expression of the radius of curvature in terms of slope $\dfrac{dy}{dx}$:

$$\rho = \frac{ds}{d\theta} = \frac{ds}{dx}\frac{dx}{d\theta} = \sqrt{1+\left(\frac{dy}{dx}\right)^2}\frac{1+\left(\dfrac{dy}{dx}\right)^2}{\dfrac{d^2 y}{dx^2}} = \frac{\left\{1+\left(\dfrac{dy}{dx}\right)^2\right\}^{\frac{3}{2}}}{\dfrac{d^2 y}{dx^2}}. \tag{2.25}$$

Replace y with z to obtain Equation (2.8).

Chapter 3

Surface Tension

3.1 Introduction

Molecules in a liquid are packed together by intermolecular forces. The net intermolecular force on a molecule inside the liquid is essentially zero because it experiences forces in all directions from neighboring molecules. However, at the surface of the liquid, molecules only experience forces from inside the bulk or along the surface (Figure 3.1). Due to this imbalance of the intermolecular forces, the surface of a liquid acts like an elastic film that tends to contract into the least possible area. This property of liquid is called the *surface tension*. Surface tension is non-directional,[1] and is described as a force per unit length along the surface and perpendicular to an arbitrary line segment on the surface. There are a variety of mechanisms that are accountable for the intermolecular forces of different types of liquid and accordingly for their surface tensions, and we will learn some of those mechanisms by comparing the surface tensions of two different liquids.

3.2 Objective

In this lab we will measure the surface tension of water and that of ethanol with the ring method.

3.3 Theory

3.3.1 Cohesion, Adhesion and Surface Tension

Although understanding all of the mechanisms that underlie intermolecular forces requires a prolonged study, it is enough for this laboratory purpose to focus on the general behavior of the forces; they are repulsive at short distances (regard

---

[1] Recall that pressure in a fluid at rest is also an isotropic quantity since it arises from the random motions of particles. Whatever plane you choose in the fluid, the pressure on the plane is perpendicular to it.

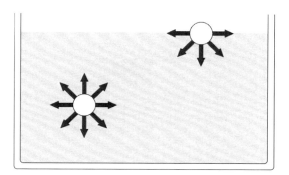

Figure 3.1: A molecule inside a volume of liquid is surrounded by other molecules on all sides, and is attracted equally in all directions, yielding a zero net force. A molecule at the surface, on the other hand, is subjected to a net downward force because there is no liquid molecules above the surface.

it simply as collisional forces) and attractive at long distances (we only consider dipole-dipole interactions and van der Waals forces). The attractive forces between molecules of the same type are called the **cohesive forces**, which play a major role in creating surface tension and holding a bulk of liquid together. The forces between the molecules of different types are called the **adhesive forces**. The adhesive forces are responsible for capillary actions, which enable us to measure the surface tension with the ring method as explained in the next section. The difference in strength between cohesive forces and adhesive forces regulates the behavior of a liquid in contact with a solid surface. Figure 3.2 shows the surface shapes (*menisci*) of two different liquids, water (left) and mercury (right), in glass tubes. The adhesive forces between water and glass are stronger than the cohesive forces of water. Therefore, the water molecules are more attracted to the grass surface than to neighboring water molecules and creep up the glass surface. It is said that the water "wets" the glass and the upward creeping motion is called the *capillary action*. As a result, its surface is curved upward (concave) against the inner surface of the glass tube (Fig. 3.2 (a)). In contrast, the glass-mercury interactions are weaker than the cohesive forces of mercury, and its surface is curved down (convex) against the glass (Fig. 3.2 (b)).

At a liquid-air interface, the adhesive forces between the air and the liquid are negligible, and such interface is called the *free surface*. At a free surface, the cohesive forces on the liquid molecules resist any external force that tries to increase the surface area of the liquid regardless the direction of the external force. The strength of these resistive forces is measured in terms of **surface tension**. The surface tension of a liquid is measured as a force per unit length acting normally on an imaginary line drawn on a free surface of the liquid. If surface force F acts along

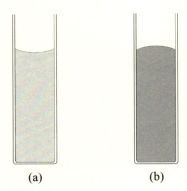

Figure 3.2: (a) The meniscus of liquid water in a glass tube takes a concave shape due to the stronger adhesion between glass and water than the cohesion of water. (b) The meniscus of mercury in a glass tube is convex resulting from its large cohesion.

total length L on a free surface, surface tension T of the surface is defined by[2]

$$T = \frac{F}{L}. \tag{3.1}$$

The SI unit for surface tension is N/m.

3.3.2 Principles of the Ring Method

Figure 3.3 represents a metal ring of outer radius r_1 and inner radius r_2 in contact with a liquid pulled upward with external force f.[3] As long as the adhesive forces between the ring and the liquid are stronger than the cohesive forces among the liquid molecules, the liquid surface is lifted up with the ring. As shown in Figure 3.3, angle θ between the surface of the water column and the vertical decreases as the ring is raised upward, and when the water column is about to break, it approximately takes a form of a vertical hollow cylinder of outer radius r_1, inner radius r_2 and height h. The water column is still at rest, thus external force f (equivalent to the net adhesive force by the metal ring on the liquid), the gravitational force on the water column and surface force at the bottom of the column cancel.[4] The Newton's law tells us

$$f = 2\pi(r_1 + r_2)T\cos\theta + \pi(r_1^2 - r_2^2)h\rho g, \tag{3.2}$$

where T and ρ are the surface tension and the density of the liquid respectively, and g is the gravitational acceleration. Thus if we measure f on the verge of breaking

---

[2] Equivalently, we can define surface tension as the ratio of a work required to increase a free surface area to the increase in the area.

[3] This method is originally proposed by Pierre Lecomte du Nöuy (1883-1947) in 1925. In this lab we slightly modify the du Nöuy ring method.

[4] Refer to 3.A Surface Tension in Soap Film for details.

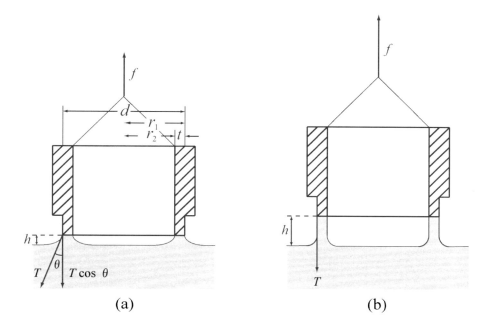

Figure 3.3: The ring method: (a) A ring of outer diameter d and thickness t lifts up the surface of a liquid. Surface tension T cannot be computed unless we determine the shape of the surface and measure the angle of the surface θ with respect to the vertical. (b) When the water column is on the brink of tearing, it is approximated as a hollow cylinder of height h, outer radius r_1 and inner radius r_2.

and assume $\theta = 0$, surface tension is determined by

$$T = \frac{f}{2\pi(r_1 + r_2)} - \frac{(r_1 - r_2)h\rho g}{2}. \tag{3.3}$$

We will use a Jolly balance[5] as our tensiometer and measure f with a decent precision (Figure 3.4).

3.4 Apparatus

Jolly balance, petri dish, weight set, pure water and ethanol.

---

[5] The Jolly balance is a measuring instrument consisting of a spring suspended in front of a graduated scale, originally invented by a German physicist Philipp von Jolly in 1864 to measure specific gravity.

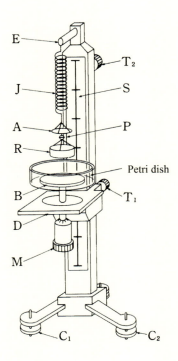

Figure 3.4: Jolly balance. A: Weight pan. B: Platform mounted with micrometer. C: Tripod screws. D: Supporting table. E: Rigid support for spring. J: Spring. M: Micrometer. P: Marker. Q: Metal ring. S: Scale on mirror. T_1 and T_2: Adjustment screws.

3.5 Procedure

1. Measure outer diameter d and thickness t of the *bottom end* of the metal ring with a Vernier caliper. The caliper is harder than the ring, so be careful not to squeeze the ring. We only need the dimensions of the thinner part at the bottom and thus do not measure the thicker part. Since the ring is not a perfect circle, measure them several times and calculate the average value of each. Then compute outer radius r_1 and inner radius r_2.

2. Put some ethanol on a piece of paper wipe and have the ring and the inside of the petri dish cleaned with it. Oil or grease remaining on the ring or petri dish would form a film on the surface of the liquid of our interest and affect our measurement of the surface tension.

3. Attach weight pan A, marker P and ring R to the Jolly balance as shown in Figure 3.4. Level the Jolly balance with screws C_1 and C_2 on the legs so that spring J and scale S align. If marker P is higher than the height of your eyes, lower it by loosening adjustment screw T_2 and move rigid support E down.

3.5 PROCEDURE

4. Turn the thimble of micrometer M to set the value of micrometer to be 10 mm. Fill the petri dish with pure water about half full, and place it on platform B. Adjust the height of table D by loosening adjustment screw T_1 so that the surface of the water and the bottom of the ring is closer than 10 mm. Confirm that the bottom end of the ring and the water surface are parallel to each other. If not, bend or stretch the supporting wires of the rings to adjust the angle of the bottom end of the ring. We begin our measurement while the ring is dry. So if you have wet the ring while aligning the apparatus, wipe it before starting the measurement.

5. Find the elongation of the spring ΔS and height of the water column h just before the ring loses contact with the water surface as follows:

    (a) While the ring is stationary, record the position of marker P as S_1. The mirror scale helps you find a proper eye position to determine the position of the marker. Position your eyes so that the marker matches its image and read the scale.

    (b) Turn the thimble of micrometer M to raise it without disturbing the water surface. Stop it just when the surface of the water touches the ring. Be cautious not to turn the micrometer too much because the metal ring floats on pure water even if you move up the platform more than necessary. Record the reading of the micrometer as M_1.

    (c) Next, turn the thimble of the micrometer in the opposite direction to lower the water surface quietly to determine the position of the marker just before the ring loses contact with water and shoots upward. Record the scale reading at the moment as S_2. Also, stop the micrometer just when the ring comes off from the water surface and record the value as M_2. Occasionally the water column stretches abruptly and then stops momentarily before the ring leaves the water surface. In this case, record the position of the marker *before* the column undergoes an abrupt stretching. From the measured values of the positions of the marker and platform, the height of the water column is computed as

    $$h = \Delta M - \Delta S = (M_2 - M_1) - (S_2 - S_1), \tag{3.4}$$

    where $\Delta M = M_2 - M_1$ is the displacement of the water surface and $\Delta S = S_2 - S_1$ is the elongation of the spring.

    (d) Repeat the measurements of ΔS and h a couple of times. We will evaluate force constant k of the spring to determine external force f in later steps.

    (e) Surface tension depends on temperature. So measure the temperature of the water in the petri dish with an alcohol thermometer and record it for future reference.

6. Replace water with ethanol and repeat the measurements. In contrast to the case of water, the ring sinks when it comes into contact with the surface of ethanol. Stop the micrometer at the moment the ring touches the ethanol and record its value as M_1.

7. Now we will examine the relationship between elongation of the spring ΔS and spring force f:

    (a) Leave weight pan A, marker M and ring R suspended as they were while we conducted our measurements of ΔS and h. By doing this, we can disregard the elongation of the spring due to the total weight of the pan, the marker and the ring. Move platform D down in order that the ring does not hit the platform while measuring the spring constant. Wipe off droplets on the ring and record the scale reading of the position of marker P while the ring is standing still.

    (b) Place a 1-g mass on the weight pan and record the position of the marker. Increase the mass on the weight pan by 1 g and record the scale reading again. Repeat the step up to a total mass of 5 g.

    (c) Plot a graph of scale reading S vs. weight f and evaluate its slope. Since ΔS and f are related as

    $$f = k\Delta S, \tag{3.5}$$

    the spring constant k is given by the reciprocal of the slope of the graph.

8. Using Equation (3.3), compute surface tension T. The density of water and that of ethanol at room temperature are given by 0.998×10^3 kg/m^3 and 0.789×10^3 kg/m^3 respectively.

3.6 Comprehension Questions

1. In step 5-(c), we recorded the position of the marker before the ring experiences a quick upward motion, not the position of the marker as it stops briefly just before the ring comes off the liquid surface. Explain why this leads to a better evaluation of surface tension.

2. Compare your measured values of the surface tension of water and that of ethanol. The surface tension of water is supposed to be larger. Describe the mechanism of intermolecular forces that yields a larger surface tension of water.

3. Do you expect the surface tension of a liquid increases or decreases as temperature rises? Discuss the reasons.

3.A Surface Tension in Soap Film

In this section we will examine the surface tension of a liquid film under the influence of gravity and derive Equation (3.3).[6] Figure 3.5 (a) illustrates a soap film spanned

---

[6] You must note that the argument in this section does not describe the fundamental nature of surface tension properly because we treat a liquid film as a membrane made of an elastic solid material. The situation in a liquid film is actually more complicated because molecules can rearrange themselves according to other forces exerted on them. However, this treatment is sufficient to derive the equation used in this laboratory.

3.A SURFACE TENSION IN SOAP FILM

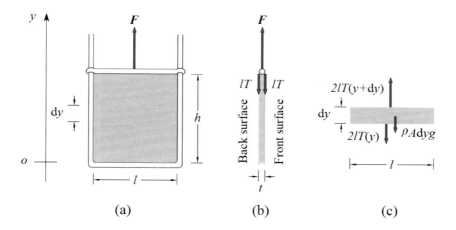

Figure 3.5: (a) A soap film expands in a U-shaped frame and a sliding wire. (b) A side view of the film. The surface forces act on the length of wire on both sides. (c) A free-body diagram of a rectangular (cuboidal) element in the film. The sum of the surface forces cancels gravitational force $\rho A dy g$ on the element.

within a U-shaped frame mounted with a horizontal sliding wire of length l and a negligible mass. The sliding wire is held at height h with an upward external force F against the downward surface force exerted by the film. If we denote the surface tension by T, the downward force is $2lT$ because the the film has two surfaces, one in front and one in the back (Fig. 3.5 (b)). Figure 3.5 (c) is a free-body diagram of a rectangular element of height dy in the film. Here we assume thickness t of the film is much smaller than slider length l, and neglect the adhesive forces from the vertical frames and pressure at the top and bottom surfaces. The element is macroscopically at rest, thus the net force on it is zero. The equilibrium condition is written as

$$0 = 2lT(y + dy) - 2lT(y) - \rho A g dy, \tag{3.6}$$

where ρ is the density of the film and $A = lt$ is the cross sectional area of the film. Rewriting it in the form of a derivative, we get

$$\frac{dT}{dy} = \frac{\rho A g}{2l}. \tag{3.7}$$

Integrating the equation and using boundary condition $2lT(h) = F$, the surface tension in the film is

$$T(y) = \frac{1}{2l}\left[F - \rho A g (h - y)\right]. \tag{3.8}$$

If the frame forms a shape of a ring with outer radius r_1 and inner radius r_2, the surface tension acts along a curve of total length $2\pi(r_1 + r_2)$ and its cross sectional area is $\pi(r_1^2 - r_2^2)$. Replace $2l$ with $2\pi(r_1 + r_2)$ and A with $\pi(r_1^2 - r_2^2)$ in Equation (3.8), and set $y = 0$ to obtain Equation (3.3).

Chapter 4

Specific Heat of Solid

4.1 Introduction

The specific heat capacity of a substance is defined as the amount of heat required to raise the temperature of a unit amount of the substance by one degree, and the molar specific heat is the heat capacity per mole, the amount of a substance that consists of 6.02×10^{23} elementary units of the substance. Specific heat is an important physical quantity that not only determines the thermal property of a material but also provides us an insight into the microscopic structure of the material and the interaction between its constituent particles. In this laboratory we will measure the specific heat of metals by means of mixture to familiarize ourselves to the basic procedures of temperature and heat measurements and also to learn about the roles of the specific heat in thermodynamics.

4.2 Objective

We will measure the specific heat of copper and aluminum using a calorimeter.

4.3 Theory

4.3.1 Heat Capacity and Specific Heat

To heat up or cool down an object, heat must be added to or removed from the object, and a different object requires a different amount of heat to change its temperature by the same amount. Assuming heat Q is absorbed into or released from a body as its temperature changes by $\Delta\theta$, the **heat capacity** C of the body is defined by

$$Q = C\Delta\theta. \tag{4.1}$$

The heat capacity of a body consisting of a single material is known to be an *extensive* quantity that is proportional to the mass of the body. Therefore, the heat capacity per unit mass, called the **specific heat capacity**, is an *intensive* quantity that is independent of the amount of the material. If an object of mass m is made of a material with specific heat capacity (or simply **specific heat**) c, Equation (4.1) is expressed as

$$Q = mc\Delta\theta. \tag{4.2}$$

The SI unit of specific heat is J/(kg·K), but we will use J/(g·K) in this lab.

4.3.2 Specific Heat Measurement by Method of Mixture

When two bodies with different temperatures are brought into contact in an isolated environment, an energy exchange (heat) occurs between the two bodies until they reach the same equilibrium temperature. Due to the law of conservation of energy, the amount of energy lost from one body and that gained by the other are the same. If we know the specific heat of one of the object, we can determine the specific heat of the other based on this principle.

In this experiment, a metal sample of specific heat c, mass m and temperature θ_1 will be delivered into water of specific heat $c_\mathrm{w} = 4.18$ J/(g·K) and mass m_w in an insulated calorimeter with heat capacity C_c and temperature θ_0, and we will observe their heat exchange until equilibrium temperature θ_2 is achieved. The heat released from the metal sample is given by $cm(\theta_1 - \theta_2)$, and the heat received by the water calorimeter is $(c_\mathrm{w} m_\mathrm{w} + C_\mathrm{c})(\theta_2 - \theta_0)$. Equating them and solving for the specific heat c of the metal sample, we obtain

$$c = \frac{(c_\mathrm{w} m_\mathrm{w} + C_\mathrm{c})(\theta_2 - \theta_0)}{m(\theta_1 - \theta_2)}. \tag{4.3}$$

In general, specific heat c is a temperature-dependent quantity, and the value of c measured in this experiment is an average value between θ_1 and θ_2.

4.4 Apparatus

Figure 4.1 illustrates the apparatus used in this laboratory. **Heater 1** consists of three layers of concentric cylinders and the hollow space inside is heated by steam sent from boiling water in the flask. A metal sample is suspended inside the heater at the same height as the bulb of **alcohol thermometer 2**. The sample is transferred from the heater to **calorimeter 3** under the heater by opening the bottom lid of the heater and lowering the sample. The calorimeter is made of copper and is hung inside of double-layered **heat reservoir 4** filled with water. **Stirring rod 5** is also made of copper and is used to homogenize the temperature distribution of pure water inside the calorimeter. The temperature of the water calorimeter is measured with **platinum resistance thermometer 6** placed in the calorimeter. A resistance thermometer is a sensory device that utilizes the temperature dependence of resistivity of a material. The resistance of our platinum thermometers increases 0.4 % as its temperature rises by 1 K around room temperature. The resistance is measured with a digital multimeter and it is converted into temperature by Excel IntuiLink installed in the computer.

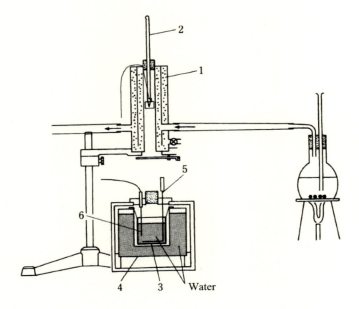

Figure 4.1: Illustration of the apparatus. 1: Heater. 2: Alcohol thermometer. 3: Calorimeter. 4: Heat reservoir. 5: Stirring rod. 6: Platinum resistance thermometer.

4.5 Procedure

4.5.1 Measurement

1. Remove any water left in the heater and the tube connecting the heater and the flask. The remaining water blocks the steam from the flask and the heating efficiency goes down. Detach the tube from the inlet of the heater and discard the water into a plastic beaker. Be careful not to topple the flask by pulling the tube.

2. Confirm that boiling chips are in the flask, and then fill the flask to 700-800 mm line with tap water using the plastic beaker. Light the Bunsen burner and heat up the flask. Adjust the amount of gas and air for complete combustion. The frame should consist of a blue outer region and a darker inner core. Once the water begins to boil, the steam from the boiling water raises the temperature of the heater. It takes about 20 minutes until the temperature of the heater gets stable. Keep the calorimeter and heat reservoir away from the burner to keep the calorimeter at room temperature.

3. Before the water begins boiling, practice transferring a metal sample from the heater to the calorimeter. Open the bottom cover the of the heater and lower it smoothly and quickly. Make sure that the string is long enough. If not, ask

4.5 PROCEDURE

your instructor to have it exchanged.

4. Measure the mass of the copper sample m, and that of calorimeter with the stirring rod m_c with a digital scale.

5. Fill the calorimeter 2/3 to 3/4 full with pure water and measure its total weight with the scale. Compute the mass of the water m_w.

6. Suspend the copper sample in the heater at the same height as the bulb of the alcohol thermometer so that the thermometer measures the temperature of the sample properly.

7. Fill the heat reservoir with tap water and hang the calorimeter from the hooks attached to the ring mounted at the top of the heat reservoir.

8. Set up the platinum resistance thermometer:

   (a) Turn on the multimeter first, then log in to the computer (no password is needed) and open "Excel IntuiLink".

   (b) Click "Agilent IntuiLink Multimeter Setting" icon in the rectangular task bar floating on the spreadsheet. "Function" parameter is supposed to be RTD (Type 85), "Range" should be automatic and "Resolution" should be 6 digits. We do not use the setting of the multimeter, so uncheck if the corresponding box (the box below the "Function" parameter) has been checked, and then click "OK".

   (c) Insert the probe of the resistance thermometer in the calorimeter. The wooden lid of the heat reservoir has three holes, the biggest one at the center is for the sample to pass through, the smallest one is for the stirring rod, and the other one is for the probe. Adjust the orientation of the lid so that the probe goes into the protruded part of the calorimeter.[1]

   (d) Click "Logging Worksheet Setting/Execution" in the task bar. Set "Interval" parameter to be 1 sec. and "Measurement Time" to be 1 hour, and click "OK" to start the temperature measurement.

9. After the reading of the alcohol thermometer achieves a stable value around 90–99 °C, it takes about 10 min. for the sample to reach the same temperature. Several minutes before transferring the sample into the water, begin stirring the pure water in the calorimeter gently for a uniform thermal distribution in the calorimeter. Do it lightly because quick stirring may raise the temperature of the water due to friction.

10. Record the reading of the alcohol thermometer θ_1 to the nearest 0.1 C°. Open the bottom cover of the heater and smoothly transfer the metal sample to the calorimeter. Do not drop the sample, for this lets the water splash from the calorimeter.

---

[1] Placing the probe outside the calorimeter is the most common blunder in this experiment. If this happens, the temperature change of the calorimeter would not be measured correctly and you need to repeat the trial. Please make it sure the probe is in the pure water because heating a sample is the most time-consuming part in this lab.

11. Continue stirring and keep measuring the temperature of the water for several minutes.

12. Stop the temperature measurement of the calorimeter. Look for the maximum value of the temperature in the spreadsheet, and record the value as θ_2.[2] An example of the temperature *vs.* time graph is shown in Figure 4.2.

13. Repeat the experiment with the aluminum sample. You need to refill the calorimeter and measure their total mass again. While heating the aluminum sample, proceed to the analysis section and compute the specific heat of copper.

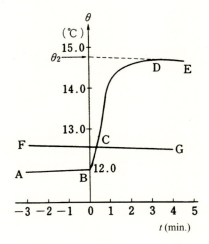

Figure 4.2: Change in the temperature of the water calorimeter ABCDE and that of the environment FG. A metal sample is dropped into the calorimeter at B and the system reaches equilibrium at D. The non-zero slopes of segments AB and DE indicate heat exchange between the calorimeter and the environment.

4.5.2 Analysis

1. The heat capacity of the calorimeter is given by

$$C_c = c_c m_c, \tag{4.4}$$

where m_c is the total mass of the calorimeter and the stirring rod, and c_c is the specific heat of the calorimeter. The specific heat of the probe of the platinum thermometer is negligible. The calorimeter used in this experiment

---

[2] For better accuracy, one can extrapolate the fairly straight part of the graph after reaching the maximum temperature and take its y-intercept as θ_2. This method offsets the effect of heat dissipation from the water to the surroundings. As for the discrepancy between the temperature of the thermometer and that of water, refer to 4.B Newton's Law of Cooling.

is made of copper. Therefore, we equate c_c with specific heat of the copper sample c and solve Equation (4.3) for c. It yields

$$c = \frac{c_w m_w (\theta_2 - \theta_0)}{m(\theta_1 - \theta_2) - m_c(\theta_2 - \theta_0)}. \qquad (4.5)$$

Compute the specific heat of the copper sample. To find the specific heat of the aluminum sample, use Equations (4.3) and (4.4) with an accepted value of the specific heat of copper: $c_c = 0.385$ J/(g · K).

2. After calculating the specific heat of copper and that of aluminum, convert them into the molar specific heat. The molar masses of copper and aluminum are 63.5 g/mol and 27.0 g/mol respectively. Express the results in terms of the gas constant $R\ (= 8.31 \text{J}/(\text{K} \cdot \text{mol}))$.

4.6 Comprehension Questions

1. Within the temperature range of this experiment, the molar specific heat of copper and that of aluminum are supposed to be almost the same. Confirm your result agrees with the Dulong-Petit law provided in Appendix 4.A, and discuss the difference between the specific heat of metal and that of an ideal gas.

2. Let the time constant of a thermometer be 5 sec and its initial temperature be 20 °C. Referring to Appendix 4.B, estimate how long it takes to measure a body temperature of 36 °C to a precision of 0.1 °C.

3. There are numerous natural phenomena that can be expressed by a differential equation similar to the Newton's law of cooling (Equation (4.10)). Name a few examples of such phenomena.

4.A Dulong-Petit Law

The temperature dependence of the specific heat of a solid reflects the change in its crystalline structure and the phase transition while it following a universal law common to all materials. Figure 4.3 depicts the specific heat of ammonium chloride NH_4Cl. It shows a peak at 242 K, representing the change in the orientation of NH_4^+ ion at the temperature. This example shows that we can tell about the structural change of a substance by measuring its specific heat.

For solid substances that do not involve structural alterations , the specific heat increases with temperature and approaches a certain constant value. In general, it is difficult to predict a value of specific heat for a specific material. However, if a substance has a simple structure, a theoretical evaluation is often available. Figure 4.4 plots the temperature dependence of the specific heat of several substances with relatively simple structures. As shown in the figure, the specific heats of the three metals vary in the same manner; they all rapidly increase at low temperatures and

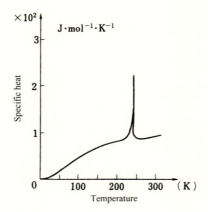

Figure 4.3: Specific heat of ammonium chloride. A sharp peak in the graph signifies the change in its crystalline structure.

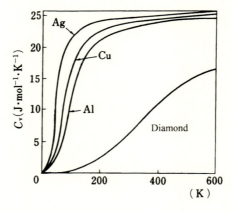

Figure 4.4: Temperature dependence of the specific heats of silver, copper, aluminum and diamond. The specific heats of the metals all behave in a similar fashion, and are about $3R$ (Dulong-Petit law) at room temperature. Whereas diamond requires much higher temperature for its specific heat to approach $3R$.

are asymptotic to a value around 25 J/(kg · K). Such behaviors of specific heat for metals are fully explained theoretically.

The specific heat of a crystalline solid is largely contributed by the lattice vibrations of its constituent particles. Although electrons in a metal make a small contribution to its specific heat, it is negligible at room temperature. Here we derive a theoretical expression for the specific heat of solids at high temperature based on classical theory.

Atoms or molecules in a crystalline solid are arranged in a regular pattern.

They are not stationary, but vibrating constantly around their equilibrium points. This thermal vibration can be approximated as a harmonic oscillation, that is, an oscillation due to a restoring force proportional to the displacement. Representing the force constant by C, the potential energy of each oscillator is expressed as $\frac{1}{2}C(x^2 + y^2 + z^2)$, in which x, y and z are the components of its displacement. Letting v_x, v_y and v_z be the velocity components, mechanical energy ε of each oscillator is

$$\varepsilon = \frac{1}{2}mv_x^2 + \frac{1}{2}mv_y^2 + \frac{1}{2}mv_z^2 + \frac{1}{2}Cx^2 + \frac{1}{2}Cy^2 + \frac{1}{2}Cz^2. \tag{4.6}$$

According to the *equipartition theorem*, the average energy per degree of freedom is $\frac{1}{2}kT$. Therefore, the average value of ε is

$$\bar{\varepsilon} = \frac{1}{2}kT \times 6 = 3kT. \tag{4.7}$$

The total internal energy of a solid sample consisting of N oscillators is expressed as $U = U_0 + 3NkT$, the sum of potential energy U_0 when all the oscillators are at their equilibrium positions and $\bar{\varepsilon}$. The internal energy of 1 mole of a sample is

$$U = U_0 + 3RT, \tag{4.8}$$

and the specific heat at constant volume is given by

$$C_V = \left(\frac{\partial U}{\partial T}\right)_V = 3R = 24.9 \text{ J/(mol·K)} \tag{4.9}$$

This agrees with an experimental fact found by French physicists Pierre Dulong and Alexis Petit in 1819, and Equation (4.9) is called the **Dulong-Petit law**. Since the Dulong-Petit law does not contain any material constant, it applies to any chrystalline solid with simple structures. However, as shown in Figure 4.4, each substance has different temperature range in which the Dulong-Petit law is satisfied.

The equipartition theorem does not hold true at low temperature due to the quantum effect of lattice vibrations, and $\bar{\varepsilon}$ behaves like the solid line in Figure 4.5. The specific heat decreases as temperature goes down and becomes 0 in the limit of $T \to 0$ K.

4.B Newton's Law of Cooling

In this experiment, we measured the change in temperature of a water calorimeter with a platinum resistance thermometer. As the temperature of water rises from θ_0 to θ_2, the reading of the thermometer does not match the temperature of water, but follows it with a certain amount of delay. Although it is not easy to estimate the actual temperature of water, we can approximately determine the water temperature when the temperature change is relatively slow.

First, we consider thermometer reading $\theta(t)$ when it is placed in water with constant temperature T. If $(T_1 - \theta(t))$ is not large, the rate of change in the reading

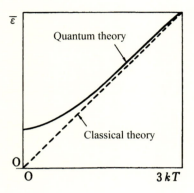

Figure 4.5: Temperature dependence of the average mechanical energy of a single atom $\bar{\varepsilon}$. Quantum effects come in at low temperature and $\bar{\varepsilon}$ approaches a residual energy at 0 K, while classical theory expects $\bar{\varepsilon} = 0$ at 0 K.

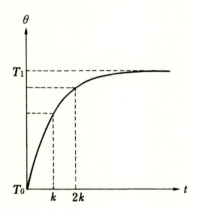

Figure 4.6: Time dependence of the reading of a thermometer $\theta(t)$ as it is placed in water with constant temperature T_1.

is proportional to the temperature difference (*Newton's law of cooling*):

$$\frac{d\theta(t)}{dt} = -\frac{1}{k}(\theta(t) - T_1), \tag{4.10}$$

in which k is the *time constant* that depends on the types of thermometers. Solving the differential equation, we obtain[3]

$$T_1 - \theta(t) = (T_1 - T_0)\exp(-t/k), \tag{4.11}$$

---

[3] Equation (4.10) is *separable*. Refer to textbooks on differential equations.

where T_0 is the thermometer reading at $t = 0$. According to Equation (4.11), the time constant is given by the time required for temperature difference $(T_1 - \theta(t))$ to reach $1/e$ of initial temperature difference $(T_1 - T_0)$. The platinum resistance thermometer used in this lab has a time constant of several seconds.

Next, we consider the time dependence of thermometer reading $\theta(t)$ while the temperature of water $T(t)$ is constantly increasing. Let the rate of the temperature change of water be a [K/s], and the initial temperature of the water and thermometer be T_0. The Newton's law of cooling is written as

$$\frac{d\theta(t)}{dt} = -\frac{1}{k}(\theta(t) - T(t)), \tag{4.12}$$

where

$$T(t) = T_0 + at. \tag{4.13}$$

The solution of Equation (4.12) is[4]

$$\theta(t) = T(t) - ak\{1 - \exp(-t/k)\}. \tag{4.14}$$

In the case of $t \gg k$ (recall that k is only a few seconds), we have

$$\theta(t) \approx T(t) - ak. \tag{4.15}$$

Thus the thermometer reading is lower than the water temperature by ak.

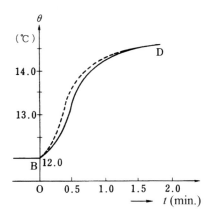

Figure 4.7: Correction of the temperature of water in a calorimeter. The temperature of the thermometer (solid) is lower than the temperature of the water (dashed) approximately by ak.

One way to determine the value of k and the actual temperature variation of the water in the calorimeter in this laboratory is:

---
[4] A standard technique to solve this type of differential equations is to find an *integrating factor*.

1. Once the measurement of the temperature change of the water-metal sample system is finished, take the platinum thermometer out of the calorimeter and wait until it cools down to room temperature T_1. Then place the thermometer back into the calorimeter and wait until its temperature reaches the maximum value T_2 again.

2. From the temperature *vs.* time graph, determine time interval t for the temperature of the thermometer to satisfy

$$\frac{T_2 - \theta(t)}{T_2 - T_1} = e^{-2} \approx 0.14. \qquad (4.16)$$

Equate this time t to $2k$ and calculate the time constant.

3. Using the value of k you have obtained and the slope of the temperature *vs.* time graph a, you can estimate the real temperature variation of the water calorimeter as shown in Figure 4.7. Note that the gap between the temperature of the thermometer and that of the water is largest where the change in temperature of the water is quickest. This correction of the graph requires a slight modification of the value of θ_2 and that of c.

Chapter 5

Specific Heat Ratio of Air

5.1 Introduction

The **ratio of specific heats** γ, also known as the *adiabatic constant*, is the ratio of the specific heat capacity at constant pressure, c_P, to that at constant volume, c_V. The value of γ for a gas reflects the structure of the gas molecules, and as its name suggests, the ratio describes the adiabatic process. There are several ways to determine the specific heat ratio, and the method we will follow in this laboratory is one of the oldest, first performed by French physicists Nicolas Clément and Charles Désormes in the early 19th century. The Clément-Désormes method is important historically as well as pedagogically because of its relatively simple procedures and its clear illustration of the role of the specific heat ratio in the adiabatic process.

5.2 Objective

The main purpose of this lab is to deepen our understandings of the laws and concepts in thermodynamics such as the first law of thermodynamics and a quasi-static adiabatic process through experiments. We will

1. measure the changes in temperature and pressure of air in a container while it is cooling down to room temperature after compressed adiabatically,

2. have compressed air undergo an adiabatic expansion while examining the time dependence of the temperature of a thermistor,

3. determine the ratio of specific heats γ ($= c_P/c_V$) for air to confirm the kinetic theory of gases, and

4. evaluate the time dependence of air temperature from the graph of the thermistor temperature *vs.* time using the Newton's law of cooling.

5.3 Theory

5.3.1 The First Law of Thermodynamics and Specific Heats

The specific heat of a gas, the amount of heat required to raise the temperature of a unit amount of the gas by a unit amount of temperature, depends on the condition under which the heat is added. Two of the most useful definitions of the specific heat are the specific heat under constant volume, c_V, and that under constant pressure, c_P. They are defined as

$$c_V = \left(\frac{d'Q}{dT}\right)_V \quad \text{and} \quad c_P = \left(\frac{d'Q}{dT}\right)_P, \tag{5.1}$$

where $d'Q$ and dT are the heat absorbed in the gas and the change in its temperature respectively, and subscripts V and P are the variables that are kept constant. c_P is larger than c_V because some of the heat added to a gas under a constant pressure is used for a work the gas does on its environment, and there is a simple relationship between c_V and c_P for an ideal gas, which is derived as follows.

It is experimentally known that all gases behave in similar ways in low densities, and the hypothetical gas who behaves like gases in the low density limit is, by definition, the *ideal gas*.[1] Ideal gases have the following properties:

(i) The internal energy is only a function of temperature.

(ii) They exactly obey the ideal gas law

$$PV = RT. \tag{5.2}$$

The relationship between heat absorbed in a gas $d'Q$, change in its internal energy dU and work done by the gas on the surroundings is given by the first law of thermodynamics:

$$d'Q = dU + PdV. \tag{5.3}$$

Here we assumed a slow expansion, under which internal pressure of the gas P is the same as the external pressure. The specific heat at a constant volume is expressed as

$$c_V = \frac{\partial U}{\partial T}, \tag{5.4}$$

and the specific heat at a constant pressure is

$$c_P = \frac{\partial U}{\partial T} + P\left(\frac{\partial V}{\partial T}\right)_P. \tag{5.5}$$

For an ideal gas, we have $P\left(\frac{\partial V}{\partial T}\right)_P = R$. Therefore, the difference between c_P and c_V is a constant for ideal gases:

$$c_P - c_V = R. \tag{5.6}$$

This is called the *Mayer's relation*.[2]

---

[1] Most gases can be approximated as an ideal gas near room temperature and under atmospheric pressure.

[2] First proposed by Julius von Mayer (1814 - 1878), a German physicist.

5.3.2 Adiabatic Process of Ideal Gas

Next we consider a reversible adiabatic change of an ideal gas. Since $d'Q = 0$ for adiabatic processes, the first law of thermodynamics gives

$$c_V dT + P dV = 0. \tag{5.7}$$

Combining this with the differential form of the ideal gas equation

$$P dV + V dP = R dT, \tag{5.8}$$

and removing dT from the equations, we obtain

$$\frac{c_V + R}{c_V}\frac{dV}{V} + \frac{dP}{P} = 0. \tag{5.9}$$

Using the Mayer's relation and $\gamma = c_P/c_V$, Equation (5.9) is expressed as

$$\gamma \frac{dV}{V} + \frac{dP}{P} = 0. \tag{5.10}$$

Assuming γ is a constant and integrating Equation (5.10), we obtain the relationship between the volume and the pressure during adiabatic processes (the *Poisson's equation*):

$$PV^\gamma = \text{cst}. \tag{5.11}$$

5.3.3 Equipartition Theorem and Adiabatic Constant

According to the kinetic theory of gases, the average energy of a gas molecule is distributed evenly to its possible forms of motion, and its magnitude is equal to $\frac{1}{2}kT$, where $k = \frac{R}{N_A}$ is the Boltzmann constant, the gas constant R divided by the Avogadro's number N_A. This is called the equipartition theorem. Monoatomic gases such as He, Ne, Ar, only has translational motion in three dimensions and their degree of freedom is 3. The specific heat under constant volume is

$$c_V = \frac{d}{dT}\left(\frac{3}{2}kTN_A\right) = \frac{3}{2}kN_A = \frac{3}{2}R. \tag{5.12}$$

On the other hand, diatomic gases such as N_2, O_2, H_2 can rotate in the surface of a sphere around their center of masses. This requires additional 2 degrees of freedom, and their specific heat is

$$c_V = \frac{5}{2}kN_A = \frac{5}{2}R. \tag{5.13}$$

The specific heat ratio for monoatomic gases is given by

$$\gamma = \frac{5}{2}R \bigg/ \frac{3}{2}R = 1.67, \tag{5.14}$$

and that for diatomic gases is

$$\gamma = \frac{7}{2}R \bigg/ \frac{5}{2}R = 1.4. \tag{5.15}$$

You should note that a two particle system, in principle, has six degrees of freedom (three degrees of freedom carried by each particle). The degree of freedom we have ignored is the elongation and contraction of the system, in which each constituent particle oscillates against each other. Such motion is modeled by two particles coupled by a spring and its specific heat is described by the Einstein theory of specific heats.[3] Although the influence of oscillation comes in at high temperature for heavy diatomic particles (corresponding to oscillators with low frequencies), its contribution is negligible for relatively light diatomic particles such as N_2 and O_2 at room temperature.

5.3.4 Clément-Désormes Method

The Clément-Désormes method consists of a quasi-static adiabatic expansion followed by an isochoric (a constant volume) process as shown in Figure 5.1. After pressurizing a fixed amount of air by $h_1 = P_1 - P_0$ and having it reach a thermal equilibrium with the surroundings of temperature T_1, we have the bulk of air follow the pass A→B→C:

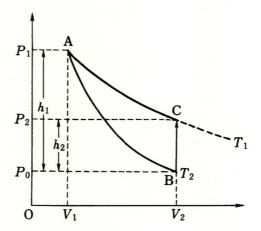

Figure 5.1: *P-V* diagram for a fixed amount of gas undergoing the Clément-Désormes process represented as A→B→C. A→B: Adiabatic expansion. B→C: Isochoric (isovolumetric) heating. A and C are on an isothermal curve.

---

[3] Einstein's model of specific heats treats a solid sample as independent quantum harmonic oscillators with the same frequency. Recall the fact that a coupled oscillator is equivalent to a simple harmonic oscillator with a reduced mass.

5.3 THEORY

1. A→B: After having a fixed amount of air pressurized to a pressure $h_1 = P_1 - P_0$ higher than atmospheric pressure P_0, cock A is opened to let the compressed air eject into the atmosphere. This expansion of the gas takes place almost instantaneously and heat exchange through the container is negligible. Therefore, this process is approximately adiabatic. During the process pressure decreases to P_1 to P_0 and temperature from T_1 to T_2.

2. B→C: The air in the container absorbs heat from the surroundings till it reaches room temperature T_1. At the same time, its pressure increases from P_0 to P_2 by $h_2 = P_2 - P_0$.[4)]

Since Process 1 is considered to be an adiabatic process, the Poisson's law holds:

$$P_1 V_1^\gamma = P_0 V_2^\gamma. \tag{5.16}$$

A and C are at the same temperature. The Boyle's law tells us

$$P_1 V_1 = P_2 V_2. \tag{5.17}$$

Combining Equations (5.16) and (5.17), and removing V_1 and V_2, we obtain

$$\gamma = \frac{\ln P_1 - \ln P_0}{\ln P_1 - \ln P_2}. \tag{5.18}$$

In this experiment, $h_1 = P_1 - P_0 \ll P_0$ and $h_2 = P_2 - P_0 \ll P_0$. The right hand side of Equation (5.18) is approximated as

$$\ln P_1 - \ln P_0 = \ln\left(1 + \frac{h_1}{P_0}\right) \cong \frac{h_1}{P_0} \tag{5.19}$$

$$\ln P_1 - \ln P_2 = \ln\left(1 + \frac{h_1}{P_0}\right) - \ln\left(1 + \frac{h_2}{P_0}\right) \cong \frac{h_1}{P_0} - \frac{h_2}{P_0}. \tag{5.20}$$

Using this approximation, the adiabatic constant is expressed as

$$\gamma = \frac{h_1}{h_1 - h_2}. \tag{5.21}$$

Therefore, we only need to measure pressure differences h_1 and h_2 to determine γ. The temperature drop during process A→B is calculated from the ideal gas state equations at B and C,

$$P_0 V_2 = nRT_2, \quad P_2 V_2 = nRT_1. \tag{5.22}$$

Combining these, the temperature drop during the adiabatic process is

$$T_1 - T_2 = \frac{h_2}{P_0 + h_2} T_1. \tag{5.23}$$

[4)] Since a part of the compressed gas is released from the container during A→B, only the rest part of volume V_2 left in the container is used during B→C. This does not affect the result because temperature and pressure are both intensive variables that do not depend on the size of a system, and the system reaches the same state regardless its size as long as its initial condition is identical and it undergoes the same process.

5.4 Apparatus

5.4.1 Gas Container

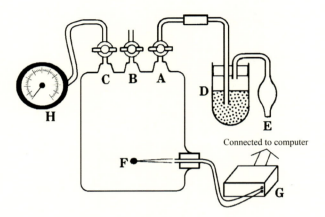

Figure 5.2: Apparatus used in Clément-Désormes experiment. **A**, **B** and **C**: Stopcocks. **D**: Desiccant. **E**: Pump. **F**: Thermistor thermometer. **G**: Temperature data logger.

Our laboratory apparatus illustrated in Figure 5.2 is a 14-l glass vessel with three tubes attached to it. The tubes can be opened or closed as necessary by turning stopcocks **A**, **B** and **C** to a vertical position or a horizontal position. **A** is connected to cylinder **D** containing a drying agent (silica gel) and to rubber pump **E**. **B** is a vent that allows a pressurized gas ejects from the container. **C** is connected to differential pressure gauge **H**. **F** is a thermistor temperature sensor connected to digital multimeter **G** and a computer.

5.4.2 Differential Pressure Gauge

A differential pressure gauge is a device to measure the pressure difference of a gas from the atmospheric pressure. The gauge in this laboratory utilizes a silicone membrane, its range is 0–10 kPa, and its hysteresis is less than 1% within the range. The gauge shows the pressure difference in two units, one in kPa and the other in millimeter of water (mmH_2O). A millimeter of water is defined as a pressure required to support a water column with a height of 1 mm, and can be converted to a millimeter of mercury by dividing a value in mmH_2O by 13.5, the ratio of the density of mercury to that of water.

5.4.3 Thermistor

A thermistor is a type of semiconductor whose resistance changes greatly with temperature. Due to this property we can measure temperature by measuring the resistance of the thermistor. The resistance of the thermistor in this laboratory decreases with temperature around room temperature.

5.5 Procedure

1. Turn on the digital multimeter.

2. Turn on the computer, open Excel IntuiLink, and start plotting the resistance vs. time graph. It continuously measures the resistance of the thermistor with a fixed interval till you hit the stop button. Leave it until you finish a set of measurements.

3. Confirm that cocks **A**, **B** and **C** are all open (vertical), and pump in dry air into the container through **A**. Close cock **B**, pump air until the differential pressure gauge reading reaches 600–700 mmH$_2$O[5] and then close cock **A**. Letting the moment the cock is closed be $t = 0$, measure the pressure difference $h = P - P_0$ every 10 seconds at first, then every 30 seconds after the change of the pressure difference apparently stops. Continue the measurement for about three minutes. Plot pressure difference h vs. time t graph as Figure 5.3. If the pressure does not get stable in several minutes, most likely there is air leakage at the cock. Ask your instructor if this happens.

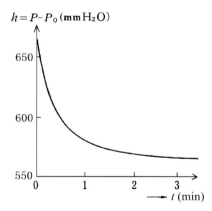

Figure 5.3: Time dependence of pressure difference h after being pressurized adiabatically.

4. Confirm that the graph of the thermistor resistance has reached an equilibrium and then record the value of the differential pressure gauge as h_1.

---

[5] If a gas is pressurized unnecessarily, it may damage the container. Be cautious not to raise the pressure above 700 mmH$_2$O.

5. Open cock **B**, close it immediately after the hissing sound stops, and then wait until the reading of the differential pressure gauge and the graph of the thermistor resistance both become constant.

6. Record the value of the differential pressure gauge as h_2.

7. Stop the resistance graph. Using the graph plotting software (Origin) installed in the computer, convert the resistance value to the temperature to plot a temperature *vs.* time graph. Each thermistor has different dimensions and reacts differently to the change in its surrounding temperature. Therefore, you need to use a conversion formula that is specific to the thermistor you used. The formula is given on a laminated sheet of paper on your table.

8. Plugging the values of h_1 and h_2 into Equation (5.21), evaluate the value of γ. Also, obtain T_1 from the temperature *vs.* time graph and atmospheric pressure P_0 from the barometer in the laboratory, and then determine temperature drop $T_1 - T_2$ during the adiabatic expression using Equation (5.23).

9. Repeat Steps 3 to 8 several times. However, you do not need to examine the time dependence of the pressure difference on Step 3 again. To examine the sources of errors, change the manner you open and close cock **B** on Step 5. Try, for example, closing the cock several seconds after the hissing sound stops, or opening the cock only slightly to let the air eject slowly.

10. Once you finish your measurements, open all cocks **A**, **B** and **C**.

5.6 Comprehension Questions

1. Discuss why a thermistor is used instead of an alcohol thermometer in this laboratory.

2. The experimental values of γ are typically lower than 1.4. Consider the reasons. If we assume that the deviation of your measured γ from 1.4 is caused solely by the exchange of heat through the container during the adiabatic process A→B in Figure 5.1, by what amount was your measured T_2 above the one obtained under an ideal condition? Figure out how we can minimize the effect of the heat exchange during the adiabatic process.

3. The value of $T_1 - T_2$ obtained directly from the temperature *vs.* time graph and that computed from Equation (5.23) is supposed to be significantly off. Which is supposed to be more accurate? Determine the sources of errors that caused the inconsistency.

5.A Evaluation of the Temperature Change of Air

The discrepancy between $T_1 - T_2$ obtained from the graph and the calculated value (refer to Comprehension Question 3) is due to the response time (described in terms

5.A EVALUATION OF THE TEMPERATURE CHANGE OF AIR

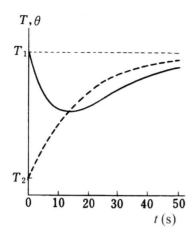

Figure 5.4: Time dependence of the temperature of air (dashed line) and that of the thermistor (solid line) for $a = 17.4$ s and $k = 10$ s.

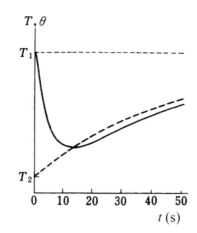

Figure 5.5: Temperature vs. time graphs with a larger container of air and a more sensitive thermistor. $a = 50$ s and $k = 5$ s are chosen.

of time constant k) of the thermistor. Do not expect the temperature of the thermistor is always the same as the temperature of the surrounding air; the thermistor requires some time to reach the temperature of its surroundings.

On Step 5 in the procedure, the temperature of air in the container reaches lowest value T_2 when the hissing sound stops and then gradually rises to room temperature due to heat flowing into the container as the dashed line in Figure 5.4. On the other hand, the temperature of the thermistor is does not drop immediately but reaches its minimum value some time (10 to 20 seconds) later as the solid line in Figure 5.4. The time constant of the thermistors used in this laboratory is about 0.5 second in the water, but much larger in the air. It is about 10 seconds if the air is stationary, and 10 to 20 seconds in a flowing air. Note that time constant a of air in a container depends on the size and material of the container, and the accuracy of this laboratory can be improved by replacing the container and temperature sensor with better ones (Figure 5.5).

The time constant of air in the container is about the same as that of the thermistor. Under this condition, we use the Newton's law of cooling and determine the time dependence of the temperature of the thermistor, denoted by $\theta(t)$, and that of the air, $T(t)$. The Newton's law of cooling applied to $\theta(t)$ and $T(t)$ yields

$$\frac{dT(t)}{dt} = -\frac{1}{a}(T(t) - T_1) \tag{5.24}$$

$$\frac{d\theta(t)}{dt} = -\frac{1}{k}(\theta(t) - T(t)). \tag{5.25}$$

Solving Equation (5.24) with its initial condition $T(0) = T_2$, we obtain[6]

$$T(t) = T_1 - (T_1 - T_2)\exp\left(-\frac{t}{a}\right). \tag{5.26}$$

Substituting this result into Equation (5.25) and solving it so that it satisfies its initial condition $\theta(0) = T_1$, we get

$$\theta(t) = T_1 - \frac{a}{a-k}(T_1 - T_2)\left\{\exp\left(-\frac{t}{a}\right) - \exp\left(-\frac{t}{k}\right)\right\}. \tag{5.27}$$

Now we express $T_1 - T_2$ in terms of minimum value θ_m of the thermistor so that we

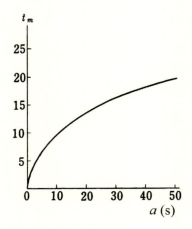

Figure 5.6: An approximate relationship between a and t_m in this laboratory. $k = 10$ s is assumed.

can evaluate the temperature drop of air in the container from that of the thermistor. Since at the minimum point ($t = t_m$, $\theta = \theta_m$), we have $d\theta/dt = 0$. Equation (5.27) yields

$$\frac{1}{a}\exp\left(-\frac{t_m}{a}\right) - \frac{1}{k}\exp\left(-\frac{t_m}{k}\right) = 0. \tag{5.28}$$

Solving it for t_m, we have

$$t_m = \ln\left(\frac{a}{k}\right)\bigg/\left(\frac{1}{k} - \frac{1}{a}\right). \tag{5.29}$$

The time constant of air a is obtained from the measured value of t_m using Equation (5.29). A graph of the equation for $k = 10$ s is given in Figure 5.6. Finally, the

---

[6] Use an integrating factor. Consult 4.A Newton's Law of Cooling.

5.A EVALUATION OF THE TEMPERATURE CHANGE OF AIR

temperature drop of the air in the container is expressed in terms of a, t_m and k as:

$$T_1 - T_2 = \begin{cases} (T_1 - \theta_m)\dfrac{a-k}{a} \Big/ \left\{ \exp\left(-\dfrac{t_m}{a}\right) - \exp\left(-\dfrac{t_m}{k}\right) \right\} & (a \neq k) \\ 2.718(T_1 - \theta_m) & (a \to k). \end{cases}$$
(5.30)

From your measured value of t_m, evaluate the time constant of air a from Figure 5.6. Then plug $k = 10$ s, your measured t_m and the evaluated a into Equation (5.30) to determine $T_1 - T_2$. Check if the result agrees with the one obtained from Equation (5.23).

Chapter 6

Diffraction and Interference of Light

6.1 Introduction

When waves encounter a barrier with an opening of dimensions comparable to the wavelength of the waves, the waves spread out, or *diffract*, after passing through the opening. The diffraction occurs as a result of interference of wavelets from different positions of the opening and can be explained by the *Huygens principle*. Christiaan Huygens, who proposed the principle in 1678, is well-known as a strong advocate of the wave theory of light, a major antinomic to the more mainstream theory of light at the time: the Newton's particle theory of light.

Diffraction and interference are phenomena specific to waves, and light does exhibit both of them. However, their observation was far more difficult than the case of other waves such as the surface waves of water or sound waves due to the short wavelength of visible spectrum and the lack of technology to prepare coherent[1] light sources, and the wave theory of light had not been widely accepted until Thomas Young cleverly bypassed these problems by splitting light waves from a single source and recombining them to observe an interference pattern in 1801. In this experiment, we will use a laser as a source of coherent, monochromatic light waves and explore the diffraction patterns of light produced by various types of slits on a screen far from the slits. This type of diffraction is called the *Fraunhofer diffraction*.

6.2 Objective

Using a He-Ne gas laser as the source of plane waves of light, we will

1. observe the diffraction pattern of plane waves through a single slit, and investigate the relationship between the slit width and the diffraction angle,

---

[1] If waves maintain a constant phase difference with respect to one another, the waves are said to be coherent.

2. monitor interference patterns by multiple slits and examine how the patterns depend on the number of slits to understand the principles that describe the phenomenon of diffraction and interference, and

3. study diffraction patterns due to two-dimensional diffraction gratings and check how their grating spacings (or grating constants) affect the diffraction patterns.

6.3 Theory

6.3.1 Huygens Principle and Fraunhofer Diffraction

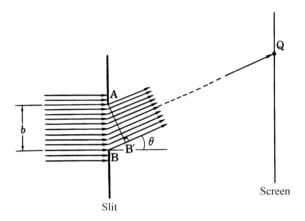

Figure 6.1: Plane waves incident normally on a single slit of width b. Waves diffracted toward point Q on a far screen are essentially in parallel and they all make angle θ with respect to the normal.

Monochromatic, coherent plane waves of light passing through a long, narrow slit as shown in Figure 6.1 do not make a sharp shadow on a viewing screen at the back of the slit, but produce a pattern consisting of a series of bright and dark bands, called *fringes*, in a region wider than the width of the slit. The intensity of the diffraction pattern is obtained from the **Huygens' Principle** (also known as Huygens-Fresnel principle). It states that

> *all points on a wavefront at a moment act as point sources of secondary spherical wavelets, and the displacement at an observation point some time later is given by the superposition of suchspherical secondary wavelets.*

In this laboratory, the distance between the slit and the viewing screen are both much larger than the slit width, and all the waves directed toward a point on a screen are assumed to be parallel to one another. Diffraction under this condition is called the **Fraunhofer Diffraction**. If incident waves are not plane waves (or equivalently the source of waves is not far enough from a diffracting object) or a viewing screen is close to the diffracting object, the situation is termed the *Fresnel diffraction*.

6.3.2 Single-Slit Diffraction

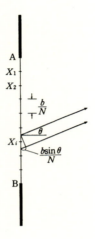

Figure 6.2: Slit AB subdivided into N infinitesimal sections of width b/N. Each section is regarded as a point source producing secondary spherical wavelets. Path length difference between two neighboring sections is $b\sin\theta/N$.

To apply the Huygens principle to a single-slit diffraction, we divide slit AB into N parts of equal width b/N as shown in Figure 6.2; here we take N sufficiently large so that each part of the slit is narrow enough to be considered a point source. Let us denote the displacement[2] of the wavelets originating from the topmost section AX_1 at time t as

$$U_1 = \frac{U_0}{N} \sin \omega t, \tag{6.1}$$

where U_0 is the sum of the amplitudes of the waves diffracted at angle θ.[3] The wavelets from section $X_{m-1}X_m$ reach point Q after those from AX_1 with a delay of $(m-1)b\sin\theta/(Nc)$. Therefore, displacement U_m of the wavelets from $X_{m-1}X_m$ is

$$\begin{aligned} U_m &= \frac{U_0}{N} \sin\left\{\omega\left(t - \frac{(m-1)(b\sin\theta)}{Nc}\right)\right\} \\ &\equiv \frac{U_0}{N} \sin\{\omega t - (m-1)\delta\}, \end{aligned} \tag{6.2}$$

---

[2] Here we are considering the displacement of oscillating electric fields or its associated magnetic fields.

[3] Although U_0 is actually a function of θ, it is assumed to be a constant for small θ.

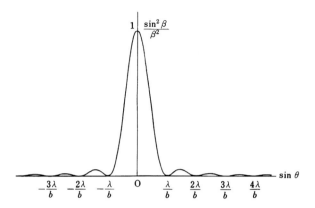

Figure 6.3: Relative intensity $I(\theta)$ in single-slit diffraction. The side maxima are narrower and much weaker than the central maximum.

in which
$$\delta \equiv \frac{\omega b \sin\theta}{Nc} = \frac{2\pi b \sin\theta}{\lambda N}. \tag{6.3}$$

Summing up the contributions from all the parts in the slit, the displacement at Q is[4]

$$\begin{aligned} U &= \lim_{N\to\infty} \sum_{m=1}^{N} U_m = \lim_{N\to\infty} \frac{U_0}{N} \sum_{m=1}^{N} \sin\{\omega t - (m-1)\delta\} \\ &= \left(\frac{\sin\beta}{\beta}\right) U_0 \sin(\omega t - \beta), \end{aligned} \tag{6.4}$$

where
$$\beta = \frac{\pi b \sin\theta}{\lambda}. \tag{6.5}$$

This result tells us that the amplitude of the diffracted waves is proportional to $(\sin\beta/\beta)$, which varies with diffraction angle θ. Since the intensity of light is proportional to the square of the amplitude, intensity I at Q is

$$I \propto \left(\frac{\sin\beta}{\beta}\right)^2. \tag{6.6}$$

Intensity maxima and minima appear in the direction where the derivative of I is equal to zero:
$$\frac{dI}{d\beta} \propto 2\frac{\sin\beta}{\beta}\frac{\beta\cos\beta - \sin\beta}{\beta^2} = 0. \tag{6.7}$$

Intensity minima

---
[4] Refer to 6.A Summation of Trigonometric Functions for details.

58 CHAPTER 6 DIFFRACTION AND INTERFERENCE OF LIGHT

Intensity minima occur where $\sin\beta = 0$, that is

$$\sin\theta = \frac{n\lambda}{b} \quad (n = \pm 1, \pm 2, \pm 3 \cdots), \tag{6.8}$$

around which dark fringes are observed.

Intensity maxima

The intensity maxima are observed at points where β satisfies $\beta = 0$ or $\beta = \tan\beta$. The former corresponds to the central maximum, and the latter correspond to the side maxima, which appear at positions satisfying

$$\frac{\pi b}{\lambda}\sin\theta = \pm 1.43\pi, \pm 2.45\pi, \pm 3.47\pi, \cdots. \tag{6.9}$$

Figure 6.3 shows intensity I as a function of $\sin\theta$. Since the positions of maxima are approximately equal to $\pm\left(n + \dfrac{1}{2}\right)\pi$, the intensity decreases by a factor of $4/\{\pi(2n+1)\}^2$ compared to the central maxiumum.

6.3.3 Diffraction by a Multiple Slit

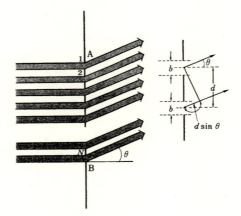

Figure 6.4: Plane waves diffracted at angle θ after passing N slits arranged in parallel.

Figure 6.4 shows a cross section of N slits of width b arranged in parallel with spacing d and plane waves normally incident on the slits. On a screen far from the slits, the displacement of the waves diffracted at angle θ from one of the slits is given by Equation (6.4). We denote this simply as

$$u_1 = A_\theta \frac{\sin\beta}{\beta}\sin\omega t. \tag{6.10}$$

6.3 THEORY

The phase difference between the diffracted waves from neighboring two slits is 2γ, where

$$\gamma = \frac{\pi}{\lambda} d \sin\theta. \tag{6.11}$$

Summing up the contribution from N slits, we get

$$u = \sum_{i=1}^{N} A_\theta \frac{\sin\beta}{\beta} \sin\{\omega t - 2\gamma(i-1)\}. \tag{6.12}$$

The sum of the trigonometric functions is calculated as[5)]

$$u = NA_\theta \frac{\sin\beta}{\beta} \frac{\sin\frac{2\gamma N}{2}}{N\sin\frac{2\gamma}{2}} \sin\left(\omega t - \frac{N-1}{2}\cdot 2\gamma\right). \tag{6.13}$$

Therefore, the intensity is

$$I \propto \frac{\sin^2\beta}{\beta^2} \frac{\sin^2 N\gamma}{(N\sin\gamma)^2}. \tag{6.14}$$

The intensity of diffraction pattern due to multiple slits is the product of the diffraction intensity factor of a single slit, $(\sin\beta/\beta)^2$, and the interference factor between N slits, $(\sin N\gamma/N\sin\gamma)^2$. Figure 6.5 shows the interference factor for $N = 6$, in which (a) and (b) plot the numerator and denominator respectively, and (c) plots the whole intensity factor. The intensity factor takes a maximum value of 1 at positions satisfying $\gamma = \ell\pi$, or equivalently,

$$d\sin\theta = \ell\lambda \quad (\ell = 0, \pm 1, \pm 2, \cdots). \tag{6.15}$$

Very bright fringes are observed in these directions, and they are termed *main maxima* or *primary maxima*. l is called the order number and the corresponding maximum is the l-th order main maximum. Between main maxima, less intense $N-2$ maxima appear, these maxima are termed *subsidiary maxima* or *secondary maxima*. Since the position of the main maxima only depends on d and λ, the width of the main maxima gets smaller as N increases. A multiple slit arrangement with a very large number of N is called diffraction grating. The diffraction pattern by a diffraction grating consists of very sharp main maxima and practically invisible weak subsidiary maxima.

An example of diffraction pattern due to multiple slits is shown in Figure 6.6. Since the diffraction factor due to diffraction by a single slit behaves like Figure 6.3, actual diffraction intensity decreases as diffraction angle θ increases, and main maxima disappear in the directions that satisfy both Equation (6.8) and Equation (6.15), creating *missing orders*.

According to Equation (6.15), the positions of the main maxima depend on the wavelength of incoming light. Therefore, diffraction gratings are often used as spectrometers, instruments used to separate light into an array of different colors, called a spectrum.

[5)] See 6.A Summation of Trigonometric Functions.

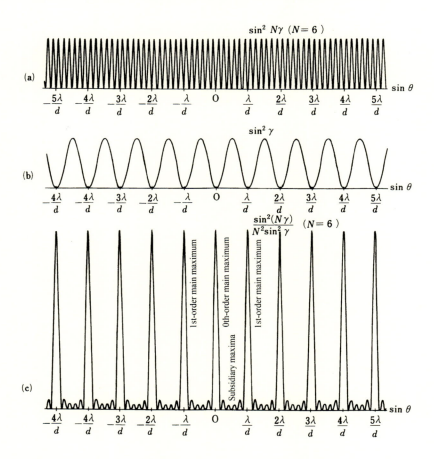

Figure 6.5: Interference factor between slits in a multiple-slit diffraction when $N = 6$. Figures (a), (b), (c) represent $\sin^2 N\gamma$, $\sin^2 \gamma$ and $(\sin^2 N\gamma)/\sin^2 \gamma$ respectively. $4 (= N-2)$ subsidiary maxima are present between two neighboring main maxima.

6.3.4 Two Dimensional Diffraction Grating

A two dimensional diffraction grating is simply a combination of two diffraction gratings positioned perpendicularly to each other. We can just apply Equations (6.1) to (6.15) independently to the x-direction and y-direction.

6.4 Apparatus

1. He-Ne laser.[6] (The wavelength of the laser depends on the color of its beam. Red: $\lambda = 632.8$nm, Green: 543.5 nm, Orange: 612.0 nm.)

---

[6] **Caution:** Do not look at a laser beam directly because the beam is very concentrated and can cause a damage to your retina.

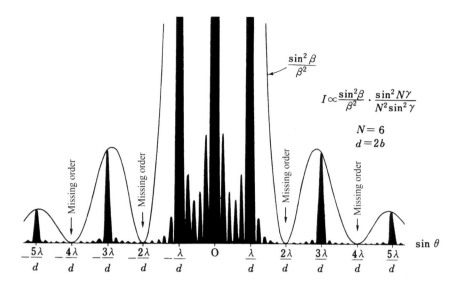

Figure 6.6: Diffraction intensity for $N = 6$ and $d = 2b$. The solid line represents the diffraction factor due to each slit, known as the *diffraction envelope*. If a minimum of the envelope coincides with a maximum of the multiple-slit interference factor, the bright fringe at the position disappears. The order of the missing fringe is termed the *missing order*.

2. Optical bench with a slit holder.

3. Single slit of width $b = 100$ μm.

4. A set of multiple slits: 8 multiple slits of width $b = 70$ μm, spacing $d = 140$ μm, and slit number $N = 1$ to 8 are arranged in a single plate.

5. Diffraction grating: 6 types of diffraction gratings with spacing d from 50 μm to 300 μm are available.[7]

6. Scanner: It scans a diffraction pattern on the viewing screen to examine its intensity pattern with a computer program (LabVIEW).

6.5 Procedure

6.5.1 Diffraction Due to a Single Slit

Attach the single slit (width $b = 100$ μm) to the slit holder mounted on the optical bench. Set the laser, the optical bench and the viewing screen so that the laser beam

---

[7] To confirm slit widths and spacings, a profile projector is available in the laboratory. Ask your instructor if needed.

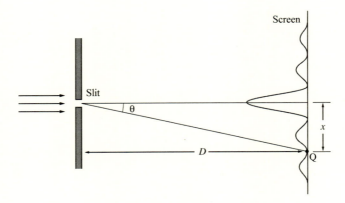

Figure 6.7: Illustration of single-slit experiment. The positions of dark fringes x are determined from the intensity graph of a scanned diffraction pattern. D is measured with a tape measure and used to compute theoretical values of x.

is parallel to the bench and perpendicular to the slit and screen. Measure distance D between the slit and the screen with a tape measure. D should be larger than 1 m. With D large enough, you can assume that the conditions for the Fraunhofer diffraction are all satisfied.[8] Scan the diffraction pattern on the viewing screen, and locate the position of the central maximum and those of dark fringes up to $n = \pm 3$ using LabVIEW. LabVIEW is a laboratory software that enables us to scan a diffraction pattern and analyze its intensity. Calculate theoretical values for the positions of minima by plugging the value of slit width and the wavelength of the laser into Equation (6.8). Since θ is small for a small n, you can approximate positions of minima x as $x = D\theta$. Compare your calculated values and measured values obtained using LabVIEW.

6.5.2 Diffraction from Multiple Slits

Mount the plate with a set of multiple slits on the holder so that the slits are in the horizontal direction. Attach a blank sheet of paper on the screen and project the interference patterns due to these slits on the sheet. Copy (contour) the diffraction patterns on the blank sheet. Observe how the number of subsidiary maxima and their intensity change according to the number of slits N by changing the slits from $N = 1$ to 8. The height of the laser platform can be adjusted by turning the screw at the side of the platform so that you can change the slits without repositioning the plate. Draw diffraction patterns for all of the 8 slits with their centers aligned. This is done just by moving the scanner itself to the side a little bit each time you copy a diffraction pattern.

---

[8] If incoming waves are plane waves, the condition of the Fraunhofer diffraction is expressed as $D > \dfrac{b^2}{\lambda}$, where $\dfrac{b^2}{\lambda}$ is called the *Rayleigh distance*.

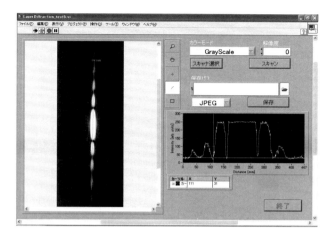

Figure 6.8: Labview screen. A scanned diffraction pattern is shown on the left. The intensity *vs.* position graph along the line drawn on the pattern is displayed on the right.

6.5.3 Two Dimensional Diffraction Grating

Out of the six diffraction gratings available ($d = 50, 75, 100, 150, 200, 300$ μm), combine two of them perpendicularly to each other to make a 2-dimensional diffraction grating. Use LabVIEW to determine spacings between two neighboring bright spots in the X direction L_X and the Y direction L_Y to confirm that they are inversely proportional to grate spacings d_X and d_Y. (Calculate $d_X L_X$ and $d_Y L_Y$ for several different combinations of gratings and check if they are almost identical.) Try several different combinations of the gratings and repeat the measurements.

6.5.4 Diffraction by Hair

Tape a strand of your hair to the slit holder and place it on the optical bench at about 100 cm away from the screen. Illuminate the hair with the laser beam and observe the diffraction pattern on the screen. The diffraction pattern from the edges of a hair is the same as the one cast by a narrow slit with the same width (see Comprehension Question 2), and thus the positions of the dark fringes (intensity minima) are given by

$$a \sin \theta = n\lambda \quad (n = \pm 1, \pm 2, \pm 3 \cdots), \tag{6.16}$$

where a is the thickness of the hair. Measure the distance between the central maximum and the first minimum to compute the thickness of the hair using the Equation (6.16).

6.6 Comprehension Questions

1. Using Equation (6.14), plot the relative intensity of the Fraunhofer diffraction for two slits with $d = 3b$ as a function of $\sin\theta$.

2. It is known that the diffraction pattern due to a narrow object such as a hair is the same as that due to a slit with the same dimensions (called the *Babinet's principle*). Consider why the Babinet's principle holds.

3. A diffraction pattern similar to that of a two-dimensional diffraction grating is produced by monochromatic X-ray scattered by a single crystal structure, where evenly spaced atomic arrangement takes a role as a grating.[9] Typically the spacing of atoms in a crystalline structure is about $d = 1$–10 Å. Therefore, X-ray with wavelength $\lambda = 0.1$–2 Å is needed to obtain a diffraction pattern. Recently, instead of using X-ray, electron beams or neutron beams are more frequently used to obtain a diffraction pattern by a crystal and determine its structure. Find the speed of electrons or neutrons with a de Broglie wavelength of 1 Å. If you need to prepare a beam of such electrons, what voltage is necessary to accelerate electrons to the desired speed if their initial velocity is zero?

6.A Summation of Trigonometric Functions

Here we consider the summation of the displacements of wavelets diffracted to a specific direction onto a far screen (point Q in Figure 6.1). The displacement of wavelets U_m from the m-th part in a single slit is

$$U_m = \frac{U_0}{N} \sin\{\omega t - (m-1)\delta\}. \tag{6.17}$$

Summing up the displacements of all the wavelets from the entire slit and taking the limit of $N \to \infty$, we get

$$U = \lim_{N \to \infty} \frac{U_0}{N} \sum_{m=1}^{N} \sin\{\omega t - (m-1)\delta\}. \tag{6.18}$$

The summation can be manipulated using the following trigonometric formulas:

$$2\sin\frac{\delta}{2} \cos(m-1)\delta = \sin\left(m - \frac{1}{2}\right)\delta - \sin\left(m - \frac{3}{2}\right)\delta \tag{6.19}$$

$$2\sin\frac{\delta}{2} \sin(m-1)\delta = -\cos\left(m - \frac{1}{2}\right)\delta + \cos\left(m - \frac{3}{2}\right)\delta. \tag{6.20}$$

---

[9] The diffraction of X-ray by a crystalline structure was first discovered by Max von Laue in 1912.

6.A SUMMATION OF TRIGONOMETRIC FUNCTIONS

The result is

$$\sum_{m=1}^{N} \sin\{\omega t - (m-1)\delta\}$$

$$= \left\{\sum_{m=1}^{N} \cos(m-1)\right\} \sin\omega t - \left\{\sum_{m=1}^{N} \sin(m-1)\right\} \cos\omega t$$

$$= \frac{\sin\dfrac{N}{2}\delta}{\sin\dfrac{\delta}{2}} \left(\cos\left(\frac{N-1}{2}\right)\delta \sin\omega t - \sin\left(\frac{N-1}{2}\right)\delta \cos\omega t\right)$$

$$= \frac{\sin\left(\dfrac{\pi b \sin\theta}{\lambda}\right)}{\sin\left(\dfrac{\pi b \sin\theta}{\lambda N}\right)} \sin\left\{\omega t - \frac{\pi(N-1)b\sin\theta}{\lambda N}\right\}. \tag{6.21}$$

Thus displacement U of the diffracted waves at point Q is

$$U = \frac{U_0 \sin\left(\dfrac{\pi b \sin\theta}{\lambda}\right)}{\dfrac{\pi b \sin\theta}{\lambda}} \sin\left(\omega t - \frac{\pi b \sin\theta}{\lambda}\right). \tag{6.22}$$

Chapter 7

Electrical Resistance

7.1 Introduction

Solid materials are classified into conductors, semiconductors or insulators according to their electrical properties. The resistivity of conducting materials is small (typically $< 10^{-6}$ $\Omega \cdot$ m) and increases with temperature, whereas semiconductors have higher values of resistivity (10^{-5}–10^{9} $\Omega \cdot$ m) that decrease with temperature. The resistivity of insulators is very large ($> 10^{10}$ $\Omega \cdot$ m) and its temperature dependence is insignificant. In this experiment, we will observe the temperature dependence of the resistance for a metallic conductor and that for a semiconductor to learn about microscopic mechanisms that govern the bulk motions of conduction electrons.

7.2 Objective

1. A Wheatstone bridge will be used to measure the temperature dependence of the resistance of a copper wire and that of a thermistor.

2. The variations of the resistances will be plotted to contrast differences between metals and semiconductors, and we will fit the graphs with functions derived from theoretical models.

3. The temperature coefficient of resistivity for the copper sample and the activation energy for the thermistor will be determined.

4. The mean free path of conduction electrons in the copper sample will be computed and compared to the value obtained from the classical kinetic theory of conduction electrons. We will understand that electrical conduction is essentially a quantum phenomenon from the discrepancy in the mean free path.

7.3 Theory

Two of the most important factors that determine the temperature dependence of the resistivity of a material are the number of conduction electrons and the mobility of each conduction electron. The dominant factor that regulates the resistance of a metal is the mobility. The mobility of a conduction electron in a metal is inversely proportional to the absolute temperature T and this leads to a positive temperature coefficient of resistivity that is independent of the temperature. On the other hand, the resistance of a semiconductor is dominated by the number of conduction electrons, which yields the resistance proportional to $\exp\left(\frac{Q}{k_\mathrm{B}T}\right)$. Here k_B is the Boltzmann constant and Q is called the **activation energy** of the semiconductor. Although it requires the band theory and the quantum statistical mechanics to fully understand the mechanisms behind electrical conduction, we limit ourselves to simple qualitative explanations derived mainly from classical physics. The basic mechanism of the Wheatstone bridge will also be explained.

7.3.1 Electrical Resistance of Metals

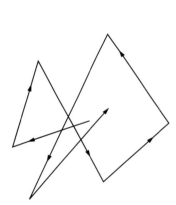 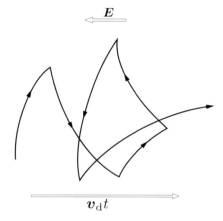

Figure 7.1: Trajectory of a free electron scattering off positive ions. In the absence of an electric field, there is no net drifting motion.

Figure 7.2: Trajectory of an electron in an electric field. The electron steadily drifts in the direction of $-\mathbf{E}$.

A part of the valence electrons in a metallic substance are detached from individual atoms and free to move throughout the whole volume of the metal, while the remaining electrons are tightly bound to each nucleus, forming an metallic ion. These free electrons act as current carriers, and they are called *conduction electrons*. The conduction electrons are considered to undergo thermal motions, collide with the positive ions and scatter off in random directions. Therefore, the net average velocity is zero if there is no external electric field applied to the metal as shown in Figure 7.1. If an electric field is applied to the metal, the conduction electrons are accelerated to the direction of $-\mathbf{E}$ between collisions as depicted in Figure 7.2. Therefore, the current flows in the direction of the field. According to the Newton's second law, the acceleration of a conduction electron of mass m in an electric field of magnitude E is

$$\boldsymbol{a} = -\frac{e\boldsymbol{E}}{m}. \tag{7.1}$$

The average time interval between two successive collisions of an electron is called the *mean free time* (or relaxation time) and represented by τ,[1] and an average electron gains **drift velocity** $\boldsymbol{a}\tau$ during this time interval. Drift speed v_d is given by

$$v_\mathrm{d} = \frac{e\tau}{m}E. \tag{7.2}$$

If the number density of the conduction electrons is n, the current density $\boldsymbol{j}$ is

$$\boldsymbol{j} = -ne\boldsymbol{v}_\mathrm{d} = ne\mu \boldsymbol{E}, \tag{7.3}$$

$$\mu = \frac{e\tau}{m}, \tag{7.4}$$

in which μ is called the **mobility** of the conduction electrons. The coefficient of proportionality in Equation (7.3) is called the conductivity and its reciprocal is the resistivity. In terms of conductivity σ and resistivity ρ, Equation (7.3) is simply written as

$$\boldsymbol{j} = \sigma \boldsymbol{E} = \frac{1}{\rho}\boldsymbol{E}, \tag{7.5}$$

where $\sigma = ne\mu$ and

$$\rho = \frac{1}{ne\mu} = \frac{m}{ne^2\tau}. \tag{7.6}$$

Equation (10.2) is equivalent to Ohm's law. Since mass m and charge e of an electron do not depend on the types of materials, only number density n of the conduction electrons and mean free time τ are the factors that determine the resistance of a metal. The temperature dependence of the number density is essentially negligible in metals,[2] thus it is enough to consider the variation in τ.

According to classical theory, mean free time τ is estimated as the ratio of the distance between two neighboring atoms to the average velocity of the thermal motion. However, the value of τ obtained from an experimental value of resistivity is much larger than the ratio estimated from the classical theory. This stems from the fact that the motion of electrons actually obeys the quantum physics. The quantum statistical mechanics tells us that collisions between conduction electrons and positive ions are caused by lattice disorders, and the frequency of the collisions is proportional to the absolute temperature over a wide range of temperature except very low temperatures. Hence the resistivity of a metal is proportional to the

---

[1] More rigorously, the probability that any randomly chosen electron experiences another collision in the next small time interval dt is defined as dt/τ.

[2] Normally each atom in a metal contributes one electron as a conduction electron regardless the temperature. Even at $T = 0$, a large number of free electrons are at avail for conduction.

absolute temperature, and resistivity $\rho(t)$ at temperature t °C is expressed as

$$\rho(t) = \rho(0)(1+\alpha t) \ [\Omega \cdot \text{m}] \tag{7.7}$$

$$\alpha = \frac{1}{273.15} \ [°\text{C}^{-1}]. \tag{7.8}$$

where α is the **temperature coefficient of resistivity** and it does not depend on the types of metallic samples.

7.3.2 Electrical Resistance of Semiconductors

Non-metallic materials do not have free electrons. However, valence electrons are ejected from nuclei with a relative ease in semiconductors, and the number density of charge carriers in a semiconductor increases with temperature because more and more electrons are freed from nuclei due to thermal agitation. As an electron leaves an atom, it provides an empty state called a *hole* in the atom. In an external electric field, this hole is occupied by an electron from a neighboring atom, leaving another hole in the neighboring atom. In this way, holes move in the direction of the electric field and act as charge carriers. Therefore, we need to take both electrons and holes into consideration to discuss the resistance of a semiconductor. Since the mobility of conduction electrons μ_e and that of holes μ_h are different in general, we need to define them separately. The conductivity of a semiconductor sample is described as

$$\sigma = n_e e \mu_e + n_h e \mu_h, \tag{7.9}$$

where n_e and n_h are the number density of the conduction electrons and that of the holes respectively. A pure semiconductor (*intrinsic semiconductor*) such as Si and Ge has the same number of conduction electrons and holes. On the contrary, their number densities are not the same in the other type of semiconductors, called doped semiconductors or *extrinsic semiconductors*, which are made by adding small amounts of impurities to insulators or semiconductors.

The semiconductor sample used in this laboratory is a doped semiconductor, and the amount of impurities in it is adjusted so that the resistivity varies intensely around room temperature. This sort of extrinsic semiconductors are called *thermistor*,[3] for they are often used as thermometers. Around room temperature, the carrier density of a thermistor is proportional to $\exp\left(-\frac{Q}{k_B T}\right)$, whereas the mobility of the carrier does not experience a significant change. As a result, the resistivity of a thermistor is given by

$$\rho(T) = \rho_\infty \exp\left(\frac{Q}{k_B T}\right). \tag{7.10}$$

Although activation energy Q is a measure of energy required to free a valence electron for intrinsic semiconductors, its physical meaning for extrinsic semiconductors is not well-defined.

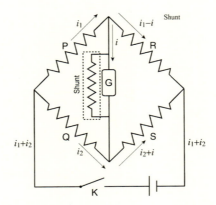

Figure 7.3: Circuit Diagram of a Wheatstone Bridge. P and Q: Resistors with known resistance. R: Unknown resistor. S: Variable resistor. A shunt may be used to avoid overloading the galvanometer.

7.3.3 Wheatstone Bridge

A Wheatstone bridge is an electrical circuit used to measure an unknown electrical resistance precisely. It consists of two circuit branches in parallel "bridged" by a third branch containing a galvanometer as shown in Figure 7.3. Denoting the values of the resistances P, Q, R and S and the voltage of the battery E, current flowing in the galvanometer i is obtained by applying the Kirchhoff's rules to the circuit. The result is

$$i = \frac{(QR - PS)E}{\Delta}, \tag{7.11}$$

where

$$\begin{aligned}\Delta &= rr_\mathrm{G}(P+Q+R+S) + r(P+Q)(R+S) \\ &\quad + r_\mathrm{G}(P+R)(Q+S) + [PR(Q+S) + QS(P+R)],\end{aligned} \tag{7.12}$$

in which r and r_G represent the internal resistance of the battery and that of the galvanometer respectively. The current in the bridge becomes zero if and only if the four resistances satisfy

$$\frac{P}{R} = \frac{Q}{S}. \tag{7.13}$$

Solving it for one of the resistors R, we get

$$R = \frac{P}{Q} \times S. \tag{7.14}$$

Therefore, if we know the values of P and Q, adjust the value of S so that the current in the galvanometer is zero, we can determine the value of unknown resistor

---

[3] A portmanteau of resistor and thermometer.

R. This type of measurement is called the *null method* (or zero method),[4] which has an advantage over a direct measurement with an ohmmeter because it is not affected by the internal resistance of the measuring device. The precision of the measurement is controlled by ratio P/Q. For a more precise measurement, choose P/Q so that the reading of S will be large and have more significant digits. In practice, it is convenient to choose

$$\frac{P}{Q} = 10^n \quad (n = 0,\ \pm 1,\ \pm 2,\ \cdots). \tag{7.15}$$

In this laboratory, S can be varied in the range between 1 and 10^4 Ω. Since one of the two unknown resistors we are dealing with (copper wire) has the resistance about 10^1 Ω and the other (thermistor) has the resistance about 10^3 Ω, it will be appropriate to set $n = -2$ for the one and $n = 0$ for the other.

7.4 Apparatus

7.4.1 Resistance Box

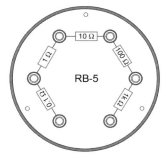

Figure 7.4: Resistance box. Two boxes will be used as P and Q in the bridge circuit.

Five resistors ranging from 0.1 Ω to 1 kΩ are connected in series and inserted in a box. We will use two of them as resistors P and Q in Figure 7.3. Simply connect lead wires to the ends of the resistor with a desired value.

7.4.2 Variable Resistor

The resistance of the variable resistor (a.k.a. rheostat) in this laboratory is adjusted by turning the four dials in front. The leftmost dial adjusts its resistance value by 10^4 Ω while the rightmost dial changes the value by 1 Ω. Numerals on the top of the dials under the pointers give the reading. Resistance between terminals 1

---

[4] A method of measurement in which an unknown quantity is balanced with known quantities so that the indicator reading of the measuring instrument is zero. Weighing a mass with a balance scale is a famous example of the null method.

and 2 ranges from 1 Ω to 11,110 Ω. The ground terminal will not be used in this experiment.

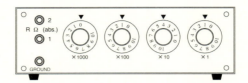

Figure 7.5: Variable Resistor. The resistance between terminals 1 and 2 can be adjusted in the range from 1 to about 10^4 Ω.

7.4.3 Galvanometer and Battery

The current sensitivity of the galvanometer is 0.9 μA/DIV, and its scale consists of ±25 DIVs. We use a 1.5-V dry cell battery to supply a voltage to the circuit.

7.4.4 Heating Device

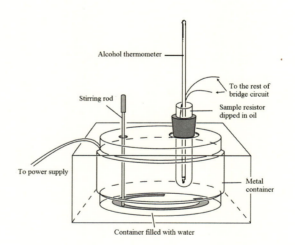

Figure 7.6: A schematic of the heating device.

Figure 7.6 illustrates the heating device used in this experiment. It consists of a copper container wound by a heating wire. The temperature of the heater is adjusted by turning a knob on the heater power control. The container is set in a wooden insulating box and an acrylic lid. A copper resistor or a thermistor is submersed in dielectric oil in a test tube for a better heat transfer. The test tube will be inserted in the container through a hole in the lid. The stirring rod in the container will be used to achieve a uniform temperature in the container.

7.4.5 Sample Resistors

Metallic Resistor The metallic resistor in this laboratory consists of a copper wire of length (3.00 ± 0.02) m and diameter $(1.00 \pm 0.08) \times 10^{-4}$ m wrapped around a ceramic tube. Three lead wires a, b and c of equal length are attached to the ends of the resistor as shown in Figure 7.7. By measuring the resistance between b and c and subtracting it from the resistance between a and b, the resistance of the resistor will be accurately evaluated.

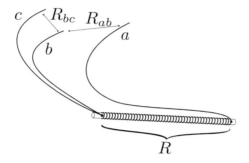

Figure 7.7: Copper resistor. Three lead wires of equal length are attached for better accuracy.

Semiconducting Resistor We will use a thermistor as the semiconductor sample. It has a resistance about 6 kΩ at 0 °C and 200 Ω at 100 °C. The resistance of the lead wires is much smaller in the temperature range of this laboratory and will simply be neglected. Thus an extra lead wire is not attached to the thermistor.

7.5 Procedure

7.5.1 Resistance of Copper Resistor

1. Confirm that the copper resistor is completely submerged in the insulating oil in the test tube. Fill the metal container with water and set the test tube and container in the insulating box as shown in Figure 7.6. You need to make sure that the test tube is properly immersed in the water.

2. Connect two resistance boxes P and Q, variable resistor S, copper sample R, the battery and the switch to form a Wheatstone bridge circuit as in Figure 7.3. Set $P = 10$ Ω and $Q = 1$ kΩ, and connect lead wires a and b of the sample. Have your instructor check your circuit before starting the measurements.

3. Measure the resistance of the copper resistor at the initial temperature of the water. Wait until the reading of the alcohol thermometer becomes stable and then record its value. Set the value of the variable resistor very small (e.g.

1 Ω), tap the switch and turn on the circuit momentarily,[5] and check the direction of deflection of the galvanometer needle. Next, set the value of the variable resistor very large (e.g. 5,000 Ω) and verify that the needle deflects in the opposite direction. Change the resistance of variable resistor so that the deflection gets smaller, and find resistance S that stops the current in the bridge. Using Equation (7.14), calculate the resistance of the sample R and record it.

4. Turn the knob on the heater power control to 80 V. The temperature of water is expected to rise about 2 °C per minute. Measure the resistance of the sample every 3 °C up to 50 °C.

5. Reconnect the sample using lead wires b and c and measure the resistance of the lead wires. Since the lead wires were outside of the insulating oil and kept at room temperature throughout the experiment, you only need to measure it once.

7.5.2 Resistance of Thermistor

1. Remove the hot water from the container and refill the container with tap water. Verify that the thermistor is immersed completely in the insulating oil in the test tube, and place it in the container.

2. Set $P = Q = 1$ kΩ and reconstruct the bridge circuit. In the same way as you did for the copper sample, measure the resistance of the thermistor every 3 °C up to 50 °C. The resistance of the lead wires is negligible compare to that of the thermistor. Thus you do not need to measure the resistance of the lead wires.

7.5.3 Data Analysis - Copper Resistor

The resistance of the copper resistor is given by

$$R(t) = R_{ab} - R_{bc}. \tag{7.16}$$

Calculate the resistance of the copper resistor for each measured value and plot the result on a regular graphing paper. Draw a straight line that fits best the data points. The line is supposed to represent the equation:

$$R(t) = R(0)(1 + \alpha t). \tag{7.17}$$

Obtain the slope and intercept of the line, and compute $R(0)$ and α in the equation.

7.5.4 Data Analysis - Thermistor

Plot the temperature variation of the resistance $R(t)$ for the thermistor on a regular graphing paper to affirm that the resistance decreases with temperature and the

---

[5] A large continuous current in the bridge may damage the galvanometer. So please do not leave the switch on until confirming that the current in the bridge is small.

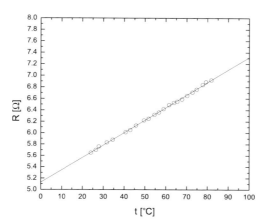

Figure 7.8: Resistance *vs.* temperature graph for copper sample. The resistance of the copper resistor linearly changes with temperature.

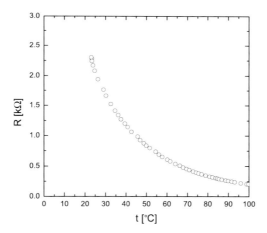

Figure 7.9: Resistance *vs.* temperature for thermistor. The resistance drops exponentially with temperature.

rate of decrease is larger for lower temperatures. The resistance of the thermistor is given by an exponential function:

$$R(t) = R(\infty) \exp\left(\frac{Q}{k_\mathrm{B} T}\right), \tag{7.18}$$

where $T = 273.15 + t$ is the absolute temperature. On a semi-logarithmic graphing paper, plot a graph of resistance R *vs.* the reciprocal of the absolute temperature $1/T$. On a logarithmic scale, exponential functions are represented as straight lines.

Equation (7.18) in the this scale is expressed as

$$\log R(t) = \log R(\infty) + \left(\frac{Q}{k_B}\log e\right)\frac{1}{T}, \quad (7.19)$$

where log is the common logarithm. Determine the slope and intercept of the linear graph and calculate $R(0)$ and Q using Equation (7.19).

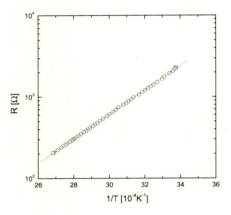

Figure 7.10: Temperature variation of resistance for the thermistor on logarithmic scale. Exponential functions are represented as linear lines in this scale.

7.6 Comprehension Questions

1. Resistance R of a sample and its resistivity ρ are related as

$$\rho = \frac{S}{\ell} \times R, \quad (7.20)$$

where S and l are the cross sectional area and the length of the resistor respectively. From your experimental value of the resistance for the copper resistor and the dimensions of the resistor, find the resistivity of copper at 20 °C.

2. Using Equation (7.6), calculate the mean free time of the conduction electrons in copper. To obtain the number density of the conduction electrons, assume that each copper atom contribute one conduction electron. The molar mass of copper is 63.5 g/mol and its density is 8.96 g/cm^3.

3. Compute the experimental value of the *mean free path* for the conduction electrons in copper. The mean free path is the distance a particle travels during its mean free time. The free electrons in copper undergo thermal motions with an average velocity of 1.6×10^6 m/s.

7.6 COMPREHENSION QUESTIONS

4. Mean free path Λ can be estimated from classical kinetic theory. If the radius of a metallic ion is R, its collision area is πR^2. We neglect the size of the electron and consider a cylindrical tube of radius R with its central axis coinciding with the motion of the electron. The electron collides with an ion only when its center is inside the tube. If the length of the tube is the mean free path, the center of only one atom should be contained in the tube. The volume of the tube is $\pi R^2 \Lambda$ and this should be equal to the reciprocal of the number density of the ions (the volume occupied by one ion). Therefore, the mean free path is given by

$$\Lambda = \frac{1}{n\pi R^2}. \tag{7.21}$$

Assuming that the radius of copper ions is 0.96×10^{-10} m, calculate the classical value of the mean free path. Compare the result with the mean free path obtained from the resistivity in Question 3.

Chapter 8

Thermoelectricity

8.1 Introduction

A temperature difference between two points in a conductor gives rise to a potential difference between the two points. This phenomenon is called the *Seebeck effect* or the *thermoelectric effect*. In a broader sense, the term "thermoelectric effect" is also used to stand for any types of conversion between temperature gradient and voltage, enclosing phenomena such as the *Peltier effect* (emission or absorption of heat at a metal-metal junction caused by a flow of electrons) and the *Thomson effect* (emission or absorption of heat due to a current through a temperature gradient). In this laboratory we shall investigate the temperature dependence of the thermoelectric voltage in a loop consisting of two distinct conductors known as a *thermocouple*.

8.2 Objective

We will measure the thermoelectric potential of a copper-constantan thermocouple at four different temperatures, melting point of lead, that of tin, the boiling point of water and that of liquid nitrogen with the melting point of ice as a reference temperature throughout the experiment.

8.3 Theory

8.3.1 The Seebeck Effect

Figure 10.18 depicts two dissimilar metals A and B joined together to form a complete loop. If one of its junctions is kept at temperature T_0 and the other at T ($T > T_0$), a current flows continuously in the circuit. The voltage that propels the current is known as the *thermal electromotive force* (thermal emf). The emf induced in response to a temperature difference is first observed by a German physicist Thomas Johann Seebeck in 1821, and the phenomenon is called the **Seebeck effect**

8.3 THEORY

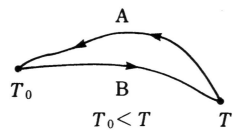

Figure 8.1: A closed loop consisting of two different metals A and B. A continuous current is observed if two junctions are maintained at different temperatures T_0 and T.

or the **thermoelectric effect**. The mechanism behind the Seebeck effect is the diffusion of conduction electrons. Since conduction electrons transport thermal energy as well as charges, a current ensues wherever a thermal conduction arises. Although electrons always diffuse from the hot side to the cold side in opposing directions in metals A and B, electronic thermal conductivities are material dependent and an uncompensated part of the diffusive motions emerges as a net current. Accordingly, it is apparent that a current does not flow if A and B are the same metal.

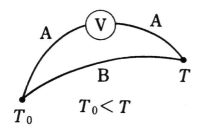 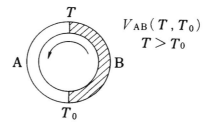

Figure 8.2: A measurement setting of the thermoelectric potential (thermal emf) and the Seebeck coefficient.

Figure 8.3: Our sign convention for the thermal electromotive force. $V_{AB} > 0$ if the current flows B to A at the hot junction.

The thermal electromotive force V_{AB} in a circuit composed of two metals A and B is measured by inserting a voltmeter in one of the metal wires as illustrated in Figure 8.2. We take an emf that generates a current flowing from B to A at the hot junction to be positive (Figure 8.9). The rate of change in the emf with respect to the temperature difference $\Delta T = T - T_0$ defines the relative **Seebeck coefficient** or thermoelectric power (thermopower) of metal A with respect to metal B. Seebeck coefficient S_{AB} is temperature dependent and can be expressed as power series:

$$S_{AB} = \frac{dV_{AB}}{dT} = \alpha_{AB} + \beta_{AB}T + \gamma_{AB}T^2 + \cdots . \tag{8.1}$$

In this laboratory, it is sufficient to retain up to the linear term. The thermal emf in the loop is approximately written as

$$V_{AB} = \int_{T_0}^{T} S dT = \alpha_{AB}(T - T_0) + \frac{1}{2}\beta_{AB}(T^2 - T_0^2). \qquad (8.2)$$

To measure the thermal emf or the Seebeck coefficient, it is indispensable to employ two distinct substances and complete a closed circuit, and this makes it a subtle issue to define and evaluate the absolute Seebeck coefficient of a single material. However, experiments on various combinations of metals and semiconductors have shown that the thermal emf as well as the Seebeck coefficient is transitive and satisfies the following relation:

$$V_{AB}(T, T_0) = V_{AC}(T, T_0) - V_{BC}(T, T_0), \qquad (8.3)$$

where C is a third substance used as a reference. This property of the thermal emf enables us to compute the potential in any combination of two substances as long as we know their thermal emf with respect to a single reference material. We normally choose lead as a reference material, and simply define the absolute Seebeck coefficient of a substance as its thermoelectric power with respect to lead. Figure 8.4 provides the absolute Seebeck coefficients of various metals. Note that they are all represented well by linear functions and their magnitudes are roughly an order of 10^{-6} V/°C.

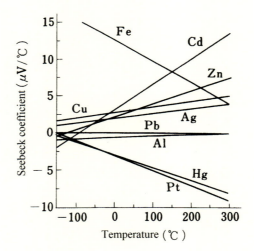

Figure 8.4: Absolute Seebeck coefficients (relative Seebeck coefficient with respect to lead) vs. temperature for various metals. Linear function $S_{AB} = \alpha_{AB} + \beta_{AB}T$ adequately describes their temperature dependence.

Once the Seebeck coefficient of the combination of two metals is determined, the combination can be used to obtain temperature by measuring its thermal emf. This type of thermometer is called a *thermocouple thermometer*. One of its junction is

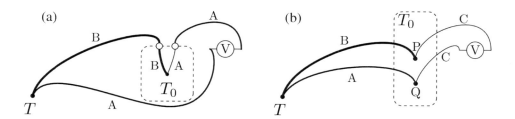

Figure 8.5: Schematics of thermocouples. (a) The thermocouple used in this laboratory. (b) A type of thermocouple thermometer prevailing in the market.

maintained at a fixed temperature and the other junction acts as a probe. Figure 8.5 (a) is a schematic view of the thermocouple used in this laboratory, in which A is made of copper and B is constantan (copper-nickel alloy). The type of thermocouple thermometers shown in Figure 8.5 (b) adopts a third type of metal to connect a voltmeter; this wiring does not affect the voltmeter reading as long as points P and Q are preserved at the same temperature. Since we can position a voltmeter more freely with this wiring, most of the thermocouple thermometers available in the market are of this type.

8.3.2 The Peltier Effect and the Thomson effect

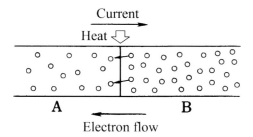

Figure 8.6: The Peltier effect. If the average kinetic energy of electrons in A is larger than that in B, electrons gain thermal energy by absorbing heat from its surroundings. Consequently, the junction is cooled down.

So far we have focused on the conversion of a temperature difference to a potential difference (Seebeck effect). The opposite conversion is also present. If two metals are joined and an external voltage is applied as in Figure 8.6, heat is emitted or absorbed at the junction. This process is called the **Peltier effect**.[1] As a current flows from A to B, electrons transport thermal energy from B to A with them. The average kinetic energy of conduction electrons is not identical in different

---

[1] Discovered by a French physicist Jean Charles Peltier in 1834.

materials, so an electron passing the junction gains or loses its kinetic energy by absorbing or emitting heat.

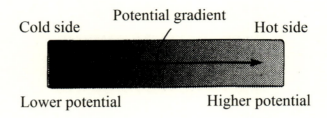

Figure 8.7: The Thomson effect. If an electron is driven by an external field, it emits or absorbs heat depending on the direction of a temperature gradient and that of a potential gradient.

The absorption or emission of heat occurs not only at junctions but also in a uniform material with a temperature gradient. While the two ends of a conducting rod are held at different temperatures as depicted in Figure 8.7, a potential gradient appears within it. If an external voltage is applied to the rod so that a current flows from the lower temperature region to the higher temperature region (electrons drift in the opposite direction), electrons need to move against the thermal emf within the rod and this requires an additional energy. Hence they gain thermal energy by absorbing heat from its environment. On the other hand, a current flowing from the hotter side to the colder side accompanies with an emission of heat. This process is known as the **Thomson effect**.[2]

8.4 Apparatus

8.4.1 Thermocouple

The thermocouple used in this laboratory consists of a copper wire and a constantan wire fused together at one end. The constantan wire is covered with insulating tubes in order that the wires do not touch each other.

8.4.2 Heaters and Heat Baths

Melting Point of Ice We use the equilibrium temperature of ice and water as our reference temperature. It is 0 °C at 1 atm. One of the junctions of the thermocouple will be kept inserted in a glass Dewar filled with ice cubes and water throughout the experiment.

Melting Point of a Metal As illustrated in Figure 8.10, a ceramic tube containing tin or lead is mounted in a electric heater. The hot junction of the thermocouple

---

[2] First predicted and observed by Lord Kelvin (William Thomson) in 1851.

8.4 APPARATUS

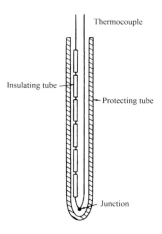

Figure 8.8: Copper-constantan thermocouple. Insulating tubes prevent the two metals from contacting one another.

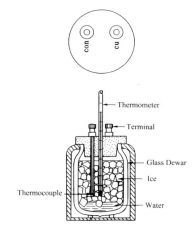

Figure 8.9: Glass Dewar. 0 °C sustained by water and ice in the Dewar is our reference temperature.

will be inserted in the protecting tube. The melting point of tin and that of lead are 231.91 °C and 327.50 °C respectively.

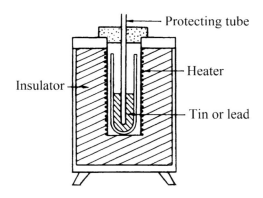

Figure 8.10: Metal heater used to give the melting point of tin or that of lead.

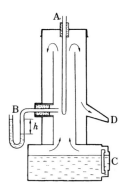

Figure 8.11: Water heater to provide the boiling point of water.

Boiling Point of Water The boiling point of water is 100 °C at 1 atm. Figure 8.11 illustrates the water heater used in this laboratory. Water vapor ascends in the inner cylinder, descends in the outer region and is ejected from D. A is a glass tube in which the thermocouple will be inserted. B is a manometer that indicates the pressure inside the heater. We will measure the difference of water levels h in the two arms of the tube while water is boiling to determine the temperature in the heater precisely. If atmospheric pressure H is known, the pressure of air inside of the heater is

$$P = H + \frac{h}{13.6} \quad [\text{mmHg}], \tag{8.4}$$

and the boiling point of water at pressure P is

$$T_\text{B} = 100.00 + 0.0367(P - 760) \quad [°\text{C}]. \tag{8.5}$$

Boiling Point of Nitrogen The boiling point of liquid nitrogen is -195.75 °C at 1 atm. Dip the probe (the hot junction) of the thermocouple in liquid nitrogen in a stainless Dewar. Since the boiling point of liquid nitrogen is lower than the melting point of ice, the thermoelectric voltage takes a negative value. Follow your instructor's direction to handle liquid nitrogen.

8.5 Procedure

8.5.1 Preparation of Cold Junction

Stuff the glass Dewar with ice cubes near to the brim so that all the cubes will not melt away during the whole experiment. Add tap water to fill the gaps of ice cubes in the Dewar. Complete the circuit as illustrated in Figure 8.12: Connect the terminal "CU" and the negative terminal of the multimeter with a lead wire, and attach the constantan wire of the thermocouple to "CON" terminal and its copper wire to the positive terminal of the multimeter. See the wires carefully to affirm that they are not in contact with each other except the junction.

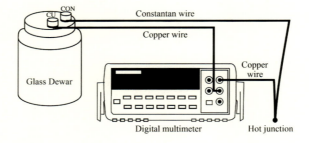

Figure 8.12: Wiring of the experiment. The multimeter reading is positive if a current flows from the constantan wire to the copper wire at the hot junction.

8.5.2 Setup of Data Acquisition System

We will measure thermoelectric voltage with a digital multimeter continuously and use Excel IntuiLink software to display the voltage *vs.* time graph on the computer screen. Check if the function parameter is set to be DCV and the time interval to be five seconds,[3] then run the Logging Worksheet.

8.5.3 Measurement of Thermal EMF at the Melting Point of a Metal

1. Turn the temperature adjustment knob (the nob on the right) on the heater controller and set the temperature of the heating coil 20 to 30 °C higher than the melting point of the metal you are using. Then turn the voltage knob so that the current in the heating coil is 6 A. The temperature of the metal rises until it starts to melt, stays at a fixed temperature while it is melting, and again begins to rise after it has melted completely. Verify this with the thermal voltage *vs.* time graph on the computer screen. Record the value of the voltage at the melting point of the metal. Make sure to turn off the heater, for unnecessary heating accelerates the oxidation of the metal.

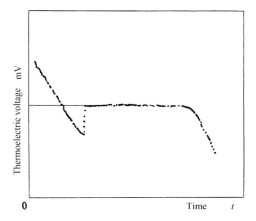

Figure 8.13: Supercooling effect. It occurs when an initial formation of crystalline structure (termed *homogeneous nucleation*) in a pure liquid requires lower temperature than crystallization around a crystal already existing (*heterogeneous nucleation*). Supercooling is observed well for tin in this laboratory, but not for lead.

2. (Optional) Once you turn off the heater, the metal starts to cool down. Figure 8.13 shows a voltage *vs.* time graph while a metal sample is cooling down. The temperature goes down below the freezing temperature then rises back once the freezing process is initiated. This is known as *supercooling*. This phenomenon arises because the initiation of freezing needs a spontaneous formation of crystals of a certain size, called *critical nuclei*, and this type of

---
[3] If you wish to observe a supercooling effect, set it to one second.

crystallization, known as *homogeneous nucleation*, occurs at lower temperatures than the freezing point, at which the growth of crystals around nuclei takes place. Observe a supercooling effect. The effect is noticed more clearly for tin than lead. Also note that it is easier to detect if you set the time interval for the temperature data acquisition shorter.

8.5.4 Thermal EMF at the Boiling Point of Water

Pour water in the water heater and heat it up with a Bunsen burner. Once the voltage graph reaches a constant value, record it. Measure the difference of the water levels in the manometer tubes and read the value of atmospheric pressure on a barometer equipped in the laboratory. Compute the boiling point of water using Equations (8.4) and (8.5).

8.5.5 Thermal EMF at the Boiling Point of Liquid Nitrogen

Immerse the hot junction of the thermocouple into liquid nitrogen in a stainless Dewar. Once the voltage becomes constant, record the value.

8.5.6 Data Analysis

1. Compute $\dfrac{V}{T-T_0}$ for each of your measurement. Then plot a $\dfrac{V}{T-T_0}$ vs. $T-T_0$ graph to determine α and β in Equation (8.1).

2. Using the values of α and β obtained above, plot a thermal emf vs. temperature graph.

8.6 Comprehension Questions

1. Consider a thermocouple consisting of a Cu wire and an Al wire. If a temperature difference is maintained between its two junctions, in which direction does current flow at the hot junction? Look at Figure 8.4 for their Seebeck coefficients. Also examine the direction of a current in a Ag-Pt thermocouple.

2. We normally connect a voltmeter in parallel with a load to measure the voltage across it. In this experiment, however, a voltmeter is directly inserted in a single-loop circuit. Explain why this connection enables us to measure thermal emf induced in the entire loop.

3. A relatively simple argument applied to free-electrons in a conductor yields the Seebeck coefficient:[4]

$$S = \frac{C_v}{3ne}, \qquad (8.6)$$

---

[4] Refer to 8.A Microscopic View of Thermoelectricity.

where C_v is the electronic specific heat. It is known that the electrons do not obey classical statistics at room temperatures, but agree to quantum statistics. According to the quantum theory, the electronic specific heat is

$$C_v = \frac{3}{2} n k_\mathrm{B} \left(\frac{\pi^2}{3} \frac{T}{T_\mathrm{F}} \right), \tag{8.7}$$

where T_F is the Fermi temperature.[5] Compute the Seebeck coefficient of copper and confirm that the electronic specific heat obtained from the quantum statistics gives us the better result than the one acquired from the classical statistics (Equation (8.16)). The Fermi temperature of copper is about 8×10^4 K.

8.A Microscopic View of Thermoelectricity

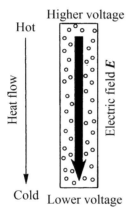
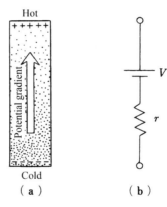

Figure 8.14: Motion of electrons in a temperature gradient. Electrons in the hot side have larger velocities and diffuse toward the cold side.

Figure 8.15: (a) Accumulation of electrons at the cold end and that of holes at the hot end yields potential gradient. (b) Circuit equivalent to (a)

In this section we analyze the thermoelectric effect based on the classical theory applied to conduction electrons. We assume that conduction electrons are freely moving throughout the volume of a metal sample while undergoing instantaneous collisions with positive ions. On the average, the electrons at the hotter region in the sample are moving at greater thermal velocities than those at the colder region. This causes an aggregate motion from the hot end to the cold end (Figure 8.14) and electrons gradually pile up at the cold end, producing an electric field within the

---

[5] Roughly speaking, the Fermi temperature is a measure of the boundary between quantum statics and classical statistics. Electrons comply to classical statistics at temperatures way above the Fermi temperature.

sample. The electric field eventually gets strong enough to stops the current due to the temperature difference and the system reaches equilibrium. As illustrated in Figure 8.15, a metal strip with a temperature gradient is regarded as a circuit with a battery of voltage equal to the thermoelectric potential in the strip. Now we shall derive the expression for the thermoelectric potential by applying the molecular kinetic theory to free electrons.

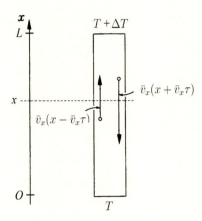

Figure 8.16: Since electrons moving toward the cooler side are faster than those moving toward the hotter side, electrons, on the average, continue to flow toward the cooler end until the internal electric field offsets the flow.

Let us denote the components of the average thermal velocity of electrons at temperature T by $(\bar{v}_x, \bar{v}_y, \bar{v}_z)$, where $\bar{v}_x = \sqrt{\overline{v_x^2}}$, $\bar{v}_y = \sqrt{\overline{v_y^2}}$ and $\bar{v}_z = \sqrt{\overline{v_z^2}}$ are the rms values. Temperature in a conducting sample varies only along the x-axis and the rms speed only depends on x. We assume that the probability of an electron that suffers a collision in a unit time is $1/\tau$, which is equivalent to state that the average time between successive collisions is mean free time τ. When an electron collides with a positive ion, the electron is supposed to reach a thermal equilibrium with the ion and scatters off with the average thermal speed at the point. In the absence of an electric field, the component of the average velocity along the temperature gradient at an arbitrary point x in the sample is approximated as the average of the speed of an electron that has scattered from an ion at $(x - \bar{v}_x \tau)$ and that which has scattered at $(x + \bar{v}_x \tau)$. Therefore, we obtain

$$\begin{aligned} v_Q &= \frac{1}{2}[\bar{v}_x(x - \bar{v}_x\tau) + (-\bar{v}_x(x + \bar{v}_x\tau))] \cong -\tau \bar{v}_x \frac{d\bar{v}_x}{dx} \\ &= -\tau \frac{d}{dx}\left(\frac{\overline{v_x^2}}{2}\right) = -\frac{\tau}{3}\frac{d}{dx}\left(\frac{\overline{v^2}}{2}\right), \end{aligned} \tag{8.8}$$

where we assumed the scattering process of electrons is isotropic, i.e. $\overline{v_x^2} = \overline{v_y^2} = \overline{v_z^2}$, and used

$$\overline{v^2} = \overline{v_x^2} + \overline{v_y^2} + \overline{v_z^2} = 3\overline{v_x^2}. \tag{8.9}$$

Electrons accumulate at one side of the sample due to this non-zero velocity, leaving holes at the other side, and an electric field builds up in the sample as well. The electric field accelerates electrons in the direction that slows down the diffusion in the sample. The average additional velocity that an electron gains due to the acceleration during the mean free time τ is

$$v_E = -\frac{eE\tau}{m}. \tag{8.10}$$

When this additional velocity due to the electric field cancels the velocity due to the temperature gradient, the collective motion of electrons stops and the system reaches equilibrium. The equilibrium condition is

$$v_Q + v_E = \frac{\tau}{3}\frac{d}{dx}\left(\frac{\bar{v}^2}{2}\right) - \frac{eE\tau}{m} = 0. \tag{8.11}$$

Hence the electric field at the equilibrium is

$$E = -\frac{1}{3e}\frac{d}{dx}\left(\frac{1}{2}m\bar{v}^2\right) = -\frac{1}{3e}\frac{d}{dT}\left(\frac{1}{2}m\bar{v}^2\right)\frac{dT}{dx} = -\frac{C_v}{3ne}\frac{dT}{dx}, \tag{8.12}$$

where n is the number of electrons in 1 mole and C_v is the molar electronic specific heat that is defined by the temperature derivative of the average kinetic energy of one mole of electrons:

$$C_v = n\frac{d}{dT}\left(\frac{1}{2}m\bar{v}^2\right). \tag{8.13}$$

The negative sign in Equation (8.12) signifies that the electric field points toward the cooler end (opposite the temperature gradient). The thermoelectric potential built up in the sample is

$$V = -\int_0^L E\,dx = \frac{C_v}{3ne}\Delta T. \tag{8.14}$$

If we apply the equipartition theorem to the average kinetic energy of the electrons, the energy is

$$\frac{1}{2}m\bar{v}^2 = \frac{3}{2}k_B T. \quad (k_B : \text{Boltzmann constant}) \tag{8.15}$$

The thermoelectric potential becomes

$$V = \frac{k_B}{2e}\Delta T = 0.43 \times 10^{-4}\,\Delta T\ [\text{V}]. \tag{8.16}$$

The Seebeck coefficient $\frac{k_B}{2e}$ derived here is a constant and does not appropriately describe its temperature dependence. Besides, it is too large compared to typical experimental values shown in Figure 8.4. This implies that the application of classical statistical mechanics to freely moving electrons is inadequate to explain the thermoelectric effect properly. In fact, electrons in metals obey quantum statistics at ordinary temperatures and you need to apply quantum statistics instead of classical one. (See Comprehension question 3.) You also need to use the band theory to evaluate the drift velocity of conduction electrons more accurately.

Chapter 9

Equipotential Lines

9.1 Introduction

The electric field is a vector field, in which a vector is assigned to each point in a designated space. One way to visualize a vector field is to simply draw vector arrows at selected locations in space. A more convenient method of visually representing a field is the use of **electric field lines**. Field lines are drawn so that electric field vectors are tangent to the lines at each point and their number of lines per unit area passing through a plane perpendicular to the lines is proportional to the strength of the electric field.

Another approach to envision the electric field is to exploit the concept of potential. The work required to move a charged particle in an electric field is independent of its path. Such a vector field is called a *conservative vector field*. If a vector field is conservative, a scalar function, the potential, can be defined at every point in the field. A set of points that has the same value of the electric potential forms an **equipotential** surface, which is represented as a line in a two-dimensional space. In this laboratory, we will visualize an electric field with a set of equipotentials and field lines to explore their relationships.

9.2 Objective

1. We will investigate a steady current field in an aluminum foil with two electrodes embedded. The current field is equivalent to a electrostatic field formed by two lines of charges. The field will be depicted with experimentally determined equipotential lines and theoretically constructed field lines.

2. Potential functions along a couple of lines in the field configured above will be analyzed.

9.3 Theory

9.3.1 Electric Field and Potential

First we will go over the basic facts of electrostatics briefly.[1] The *electric field* $\boldsymbol{E}$ is defined as the electric force exerted on a unit charge. If a test charge q experiences electric force $\boldsymbol{F}$, the electric field is given by $\boldsymbol{E} = \boldsymbol{F}/q$. According to the Coulomb's law, the electric field $\boldsymbol{E}$ at distance r from a point charge Q is

$$\boldsymbol{E} = \frac{1}{4\pi\varepsilon_0}\frac{Q}{r^2}\hat{\boldsymbol{r}}, \qquad (9.1)$$

where $\varepsilon_0 = 8.85 \times 10^{-12}$ C^2/(N·m^2) is the permittivity constant and $\hat{\boldsymbol{r}}$ is a unit vector directed from Q to the point of interest. The electric field obeys the *superposition principle*; the E-field due to multiple discrete charges is computed as the vector sum of the field for a single charge, and that due to a continuous charge distribution is obtained by an integral.

One of the important properties of the electric field is that it is conservative, meaning the energy is not created or destroyed while moving a charge along a closed path. Denoting the infinitesimal displacement along the path by $d\boldsymbol{r}$, it is described as

$$\oint \boldsymbol{E} \cdot d\boldsymbol{r} = 0. \qquad (9.2)$$

This allows us to assign a well-defined scalar ϕ, called the *electric potential*, at each point in space:

$$\phi = -\int \boldsymbol{E} \cdot d\boldsymbol{r}. \qquad (9.3)$$

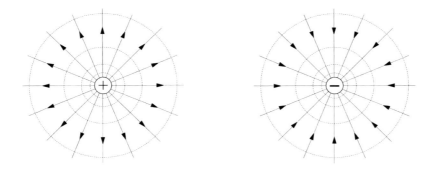

Figure 9.1: Electric field lines (solid lines) and equipotentials (dashed lines) for a positive point charge (left) and those for a negative point charge (right).

Electric fields are often portrayed with a set of electric field lines and equipotentials as in Figure 9.1. Some of their characteristics are:

---
[1] Refer to a textbook on electromagnetism for more details.

- Electric field lines never begin or end in an empty space. They originate from positive charges and terminate at negative charges.[2] In the presence of an excess of charge, some of the lines begin or end infinitely far away.

- Field lines never cross. Otherwise, the electric field is not uniquely defined.

- Equipotential surfaces are always closed unless they extend from infinity to infinity.

- Since the work done by the electric force along an equipotential is zero, electric field lines and equipotential lines are always perpendicular to each other.

These aspects of field lines and equipotentials constitute a set of crucial rules we must follow while visualizing an electric field. We will map out the E-field for a simple symmetric charge configuration following these rules.

9.3.2 Potential Due to Lines of Charges

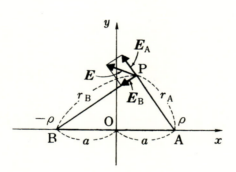

Figure 9.2: A pair of parallel lines perpendicular to the page. A positive charge density ρ is distributed along one of them, and $-\rho$ along the other.

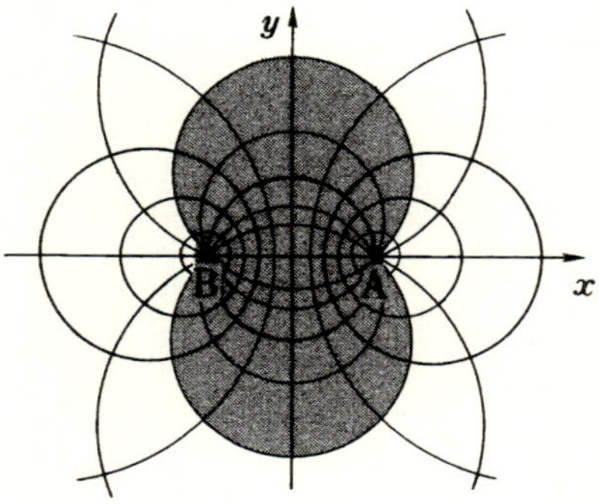

Figure 9.3: Equipotential lines and electric field lines for the charge configuration in Figure 9.2.

In general, it is difficult to analytically determine an electric field formed by a multiple charge configuration or continuous charge distribution. However, if charge configurations or distributions have some symmetry, exact solutions are sometimes available. Conducting an experiment to confirm such solutions is worthwhile because it helps us grasp the concept of the electric field more firmly.

We will examine an analytically solvable field formed by a pair of parallel lines of charges in this experiment. The electric field at distance r from a uniform linear

---

[2] This statement is essentially equivalent to the Gauss' law (Equation (9.10)): the total number of field lines passing through a closed surface is proportional to the net amount of charge enclosed in the surface.

charge density ρ distributed along an infinitely long straight rod is either solved directly from the Coulomb's law or by applying the Gauss' law. The result is

$$E(r) = \frac{\rho}{2\pi\varepsilon r}. \tag{9.4}$$

Using the definition, the electric potential is

$$\phi(r) = -\int_{r_0}^{r} E(r)\mathrm{d}r = \frac{\rho}{2\pi\varepsilon}\ln\frac{r_0}{r}, \tag{9.5}$$

where r_0 is the distance between the rod and an arbitrarily chosen reference point. If we have two parallel lines of charges, arranged as shown in Figure 9.2, the electric field at point P is obtained by the superposition principle, it yields

$$\phi = \frac{\rho}{2\pi\varepsilon}\ln\frac{r_B}{r_A}, \tag{9.6}$$

where r_A and r_B are $\overline{AP}$ and $\overline{BP}$ in Figure 9.2, respectively. Since the potential is constant on an equipotential line, equipotential lines satisfy the following condition:

$$\frac{r_B}{r_A} = C_1. \qquad (C_1 \text{ is a constant.}) \tag{9.7}$$

In terms of the coordinates of P(x, y), the above condition is expressed as

$$\left(x + \frac{1+C_1^2}{1-C_1^2}a\right)^2 + y^2 = \frac{4C_1^2}{(1-C_1^2)^2}a^2. \tag{9.8}$$

Thus the equipotential lines for the two parallel lines of charges are circular. The electric field lines are acquired as the lines perpendicular to the equipotential lines. Following algebraic calculations in Appendix 9.A, the field lines are found to be circular arcs:

$$x^2 + (y+C_2)^2 = a^2 + C_2^2. \tag{9.9}$$

Figure 9.3 shows a set of equipotential lines and electric field lines expressed by Equations (9.8) and (9.9). Note that the electric field is two dimensional by symmetry; it is exactly the same in any plane parallel to the xy-plane because the two line charge distributions extend infinitely.

9.3.3 Electrostatic Field and Steady Current Field

The electric field can be determined by measuring the direction and magnitude of the electric force on a test charge. This direct measurement is technically difficult, so we will figure out the electric field by a more indirect means in this laboratory: first constructing a steady current field equivalent to the electrostatic field of our interest, measuring its current distribution,[3] and interpreting the result as its corresponding electric field.

---

[3] What we actually measure is the potential. The electric field is uniquely determined as the negative of the potential gradient.

CHAPTER 9 EQUIPOTENTIAL LINES

For the sake of our experiment, we will inspect the relationship between a electrostatic field and a correspondent steady current field. Both the electrostatic field and steady current field satisfy the Gauss' law:

$$\oint_s \varepsilon \boldsymbol{E} \cdot \mathrm{d}\boldsymbol{S} = Q \tag{9.10}$$

$$\oint_s \sigma \boldsymbol{E} \cdot \mathrm{d}\boldsymbol{S} = I, \tag{9.11}$$

in which Q is the net electric charge inside the closed surface, I is the net current originates inside the surface, and ε and σ are permittivity and conductivity respectively. From these equations, it is apparent that an electrostatic field and a steady current field have the following correspondence:

Static field	Steady current field
$\boldsymbol{E}$	$\boldsymbol{E}$
ε	σ
Q	I

The steady current field that corresponds to the static field due to the two parallel lines of charges shown in Figure 9.2 is the one formed by the current in a infinite conducting plane with two electrodes mounted at points A and B. Suppose that current I originates from electrode A, flows in a conducting plate with conductivity σ and terminates at electrode B, the steady current field is exactly the same as the electrostatic field if Q and I obey the following relationship:

$$\frac{Q}{\varepsilon} = \frac{I}{\sigma}. \tag{9.12}$$

If the thickness of the conducting sheet is δ, the charge Q is equal to $\rho\delta$. Equation (9.12) is written as

$$\frac{\rho}{\varepsilon} = \frac{I}{\sigma\delta}. \tag{9.13}$$

It is practically impossible to provide an infinite conducting plane. However, if you prepare a conducting sheet whose contour matches one of the electric field lines, the electric field inside the sheet is exactly the same as that of the infinite plane. We will conduct a steady current field measurement using an aluminum foil cut out along two of its electric field lines. Note that the amount of current in this finite aluminum has to be diminished to

$$I' = \frac{\theta}{2\pi} I, \tag{9.14}$$

where θ is the angle of the two contour arcs make at their intersections (Figure 9.5). Inserting Equation (9.14) into Equation (9.13), then the result into Equation (9.6), the potential on the aluminum foil is

$$\phi = \frac{I'}{\sigma\delta\theta} \ln \frac{r_B}{r_A}. \tag{9.15}$$

The conductivity of aluminum at room temperature (20 °C) is 3.64×10^7 $(\Omega \cdot m)^{-1}$, and the thickness of the foil used in this lab is 11 μm.

9.4 Apparatus

DC power supply, measurement platform, digital multimeter, test probes, aluminum foil, tracing paper and set of stationery.

9.5 Procedure

9.5.1 Setup

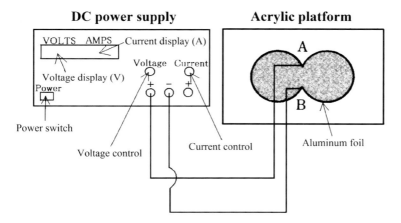

Figure 9.4: Configuration of DC power supply and acrylic platform.

Measure the distance between the two holes A and B in the acrylic platform (Figure 9.4). Draw two congruent circles with $\overline{AB}$ as a common chord on a piece of tracing paper and measure the angle that their tangent lines make at A or B. (It is possible to draw two circles with different radii, but that would make the following measurement awkward.) Attach the tracing sheet to a piece of aluminum foil of the same size and cut them together along the circular arcs to obtain a geometry shown in Figure 9.5. Fix the foil on the acrylic platform with adhesive tapes, and attach the electrodes to the holes A and B as illustrated in Figure 9.6. Make sure that the washers of the electrodes are in contact with the aluminum foil. Connect the electrodes and the power supply with lead wires as depicted in Figure 9.4. Turn on the power supply and set the current I' to 0.6 - 0.7 A by adjusting the current control. (If the current does not reach a desired value, you also need to adjust the voltage control.) Attach the hand-held probes to the digital multimeter; the red probe goes to the positive terminal and the black to the negative terminal.

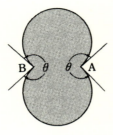 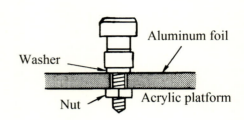

Figure 9.5: Aluminum foil cut out along electric field lines. Note that θ is inside the contour.

Figure 9.6: Electrode. The washer should contact the aluminum foil.

9.5.2 Measurement of Equipotentials

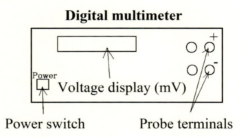

Figure 9.7: Digital multimeter used to measure the potential difference between two hand-held probes.

Put seven small marks with a blue marker along segment $\overline{AB}$ to divide the segment roughly into eight equal parts. Fix the negative probe *aside* one of the marks[4] and move around the positive probe on the foil to find a set of points that is equipotential with the location of the negative probe. Put small blue marks on those points. Keep in mind that the current in the multimeter slightly affects the potential landscape in the foil and the electric field in the foil is maintained only when the voltage reading is exactly zero. However, it is very hard to locate a position where the voltage reading is exactly 0 mV, so you can assume that two points are equipotential if the voltage is less than 0.005 mV. You need to find enough points so that you can draw a smooth line by connecting them later. Repeat the steps for the rest six points along segment $\overline{AB}$. You are *not* supposed to draw equipotential lines directly on the aluminum foil, at least for the moment, for the lines may alter the current distribution on the foil and affect the next measurement.

---

[4] If you place the probe *on* the mark, the probe may be insulated from the foil.

9.5.3 Evaluation of Potential Functions

Taking the origin at the midpoint of segment $\overline{AB}$ and $+x$-axis toward A, put small dots every 1 cm with a red marker. Place the negative probe aside the origin ($x = 0$) and measure the potential aside all the other dots ($x = \pm 1, \pm 2, \ldots$ cm). Repeat the same steps along the line that passes the origin and makes 45° from the $+x$-axis: mark $s = \pm 1, \pm 2, \ldots$ cm along the line all the way to the rims of the foil and measure the potential at each mark with respect to the origin. Record current I' on the display of the DC power supply. It will be needed for your theoretical calculations of potential distribution performed in Analysis section.

9.5.4 Analysis

1. Remove the electrodes from the platform. While the aluminum foil is still fixed, superpose the piece of tracing paper on the foil, and trace all the blue marks on the foil (marks used to determine equipotentials) onto the tracing paper. Draw seven equipotential lines with a blue marker on the tracing paper by connecting the copied marks. Then draw seven electric field lines with a red marker. Note that the electric field lines must be always perpendicular to the equipotential lines. Verify that the pattern of the equipotentials and field lines on the tracing paper agrees with Equations (9.8) and (9.9).

2. For each measurement of the potential along $\overline{AB}$, compute a theoretical value using Equation (9.15), where $r_A = x - a$ and $r_B = x + a$. Plot two potential vs. x graphs on a piece of graph paper, one using the measured values and the other using the calculated values. Repeat the same for the potential along the line that makes 45° to $\overline{AB}$. The components of the marked positions s are $x = s/\sqrt{2}$ and $y = s/\sqrt{2}$, and r_A and r_B in Equation (9.15) are, respectively,

$$r_A = \sqrt{\left(\frac{s}{\sqrt{2}} - a\right)^2 + \left(\frac{s}{\sqrt{2}}\right)^2} \text{ and } r_B = \sqrt{\left(\frac{s}{\sqrt{2}} + a\right)^2 + \left(\frac{s}{\sqrt{2}}\right)^2}, \quad (9.16)$$

where a is the length of $\overline{OA}$. (See Figure 9.2.)

9.6 Comprehension Questions

1. There is a wide range of practical applications on the correspondence between electrostatic fields and steady current fields. One of such applications is the measurement of capacitance C. The capacitance of a insulator of permittivity ε between conductors of complicated geometry can be obtained by placing the conductors in a electrolyte of conductivity σ and measuring its resistance R. Derive the equation to compute C from R.

2. We have shown that the steady current field due to two electrodes in a thin conducting layer exactly corresponds to the electrostatic field formed by two

linear charge distributions. Instead, try to approximate the electrode configuration with a dipole (a pair of positive and negative charges of equal magnitude). Does the approximation fit your experimental results well? What is the difficulty of the approximation?

3. Prove that a uniform charge distribution on the surface of an infinitely long cylinder produces the same electric field as an infinitely long line of charge. This implies that cylindrical electrodes yield the same steady current field as those in the shape of a thin rod.

9.A Derivation of Electric Field Lines

In this section, we will derive Equation (9.9) from Equation (9.8). The slope of the equipotential line at position (x, y) is given by the derivative of Equation (9.8). We have

$$\frac{dy}{dx} = -\frac{1}{y}\left(x - \frac{1 + C_1^2}{1 - C_1^2}a\right). \tag{9.17}$$

Since the electric field lines are perpendicular to the equipotentials, the field line passing through this point should have the derivative

$$\frac{dy}{dx} = \frac{y}{x + \frac{1 + C_1^2}{1 - C_1^2}a}. \tag{9.18}$$

Recalling that $C_1 = \frac{r_B}{r_A}$, we plug

$$\frac{(x + a)^2 + y^2}{(x - a)^2 + y^2} = C_1^2 \tag{9.19}$$

into Equation (9.18) and arrange in the descending order of x. The equation reduces to

$$\frac{x^2}{y^2} - \frac{2x}{y}\frac{dx}{dy} = 1 + \frac{a^2}{y^2}. \tag{9.20}$$

Since the left hand side of this equation is equal to

$$-\frac{d}{dy}\left(\frac{x^2}{y}\right), \tag{9.21}$$

we can directly integrate Equation (9.20). It becomes

$$-\frac{x^2}{y} = y - \frac{a^2}{y} + 2C_2. \qquad (C_2 \text{ is a constant.}) \tag{9.22}$$

Rearrange it to obtain Equation (9.9).

Chapter 10

AC Circuits and Resonance

10.1 Introduction

Electrical and electronic circuits[1] constitute indispensable parts in modern society and are ingrained in almost every part of our daily lives. Household appliances, phones, computers, trains, just to name a few, are all driven and regulated by electric and/or electronic circuits. Although modern electronic circuits heavily depend on semiconducting components such as diode and transistor, they also require more basic elements, resistors, capacitors and inductors to function properly. In this lab, we will investigate resonance in alternating current (AC) circuits consisting of these three simple elements to achieve a deeper understanding of the basics of electrical circuits. Resonance is an important phenomenon observed in a variety of physical systems, and learning it is another goal of this experiment.

10.2 Objective

1. Resonance in a series LC circuit will be observed. We will vary the frequency of the applied voltage around its resonant frequency and measure the current to plot a resonance curve. From the curve, the Q factor of the circuit, a measure of the sharpness of resonance, will be determined and the physical quantities that affect the Q factor will be analyzed.

2. The response of a parallel LC circuit to the variation in frequency of the driving voltage will be studied.

---

[1] Electrical circuits are circuits employed to store electrical energy or to convert it into other forms of energy, such as mechanical energy or thermal energy. On the other hand, circuits used to control electrical signals are called electronic circuits.

10.3 Theory

10.3.1 Resistor, Capacitor and Inductor

In a direct current (DC) circuit, a continuous current does not flow in a capacitor-containing circuit, and the amount of current in the circuit is controlled solely by the combination of resistors. However, in an AC circuit, current flows continuously even if it involves a capacitor and it can be used to regulate current. In addition, an inductor in an AC circuit also affects current through electromagnetic induction. Resistors, capacitors and inductors are the most fundamental components in electrical circuits, and we first discuss the relationship between current I in each of these components and voltage V across it. Here we treat sinusoidal currents and voltages, which are considered most essential.[2] The relationship between I [A] and

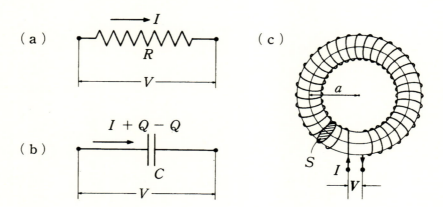

Figure 10.1: (a) The voltage across a resistor is proportional to the current in the resistor: $V = IR$. (b) The voltage across a capacitor is proportional to the charge stored in it: $V = Q/C$. (c) Toroidal inductor of radius a and cross section S. The voltage across an inductor is proportional to the rate of change in the current: $V = L \, dI/dt$.

V [V] for a resistor (Figure 10.1 (a)) in an AC circuit is given by Ohm's law just like in a DC circuit:

$$V = RI. \tag{10.1}$$

If a sinusoidal voltage $V = V_0 \cos \omega t$ is applied to the resistor, the current in the resistor is

$$I = \frac{V_0}{R} \cos \omega t = I_0 \cos \omega t. \tag{10.2}$$

---

[2] Periodic signals in any other forms, in principle, can be constructed by superposing sinusoidal signals.

10.3 THEORY

Thus *the voltage across a resistor is in phase with the current*, and the resistance gives the ratio of the maximum voltage V_0 to the maximum current I_0.

Charge Q [C] stored in a capacitor (Figure 10.1 (b)) at one moment is described in terms of its capacitance C [F] as

$$Q = CV. \tag{10.3}$$

The rate of change in its stored charge is the current flowing into the capacitor. Therefore, we have

$$\frac{dQ}{dt} = I = C\frac{dV}{dt}. \tag{10.4}$$

For $V = V_0 \cos \omega t$, the current into the capacitor is

$$I = -C\omega V_0 \sin \omega t = I_0 \cos\left(\omega t + \frac{\pi}{2}\right). \tag{10.5}$$

The equation tells us that *the voltage across a capacitor lags the current by $\frac{\pi}{2}$* (the current leads the voltage). The maximum voltage and current are related as

$$V_0 = \left(\frac{1}{\omega C}\right) I_0. \tag{10.6}$$

The ratio $\dfrac{1}{\omega C}$ is called the **capacitive reactance** and it plays a role similar to resistance.

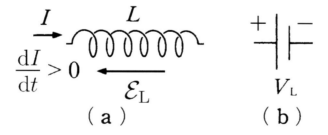

Figure 10.2: Voltage across an inductor. (a) Induced emf impedes the increase in current. (b) Battery equivalent to the inductor at the moment.

An inductor is a conducting wire closely wrapped around a ferromagnetic core. We consider a n-turn coil wound around a circular ring of radius a [m] and cross section S [m^2] as illustrated in Figure 10.1 (c). This conformation is called a *toroid*. If the current in the inductor is I, the magnetic field strength H [A/m] inside the coil is obtained from Ampère's law:

$$H \cdot 2\pi a = nI. \tag{10.7}$$

Denoting the permeability of the circular ring by μ [H/m], the magnetic field B is

$$B = \mu H = \frac{\mu n I}{2\pi a}. \tag{10.8}$$

The total magnetic flux through the coil is calculated as

$$\Phi = nBS = \frac{\mu n^2 S I}{2\pi a} = LI, \tag{10.9}$$

where

$$L = \frac{\mu n^2 S}{2\pi a} \tag{10.10}$$

is the self-inductance of the coil (its unit is henry [H]). Although the self-inductance itself depends on the geometry and core material of the inductor, the proportionality between the flux and current is a general property of inductors. According to Faraday's law of electromagnetic induction, the induced emf due to the self-induction of the coil $\mathcal{E}_L$ is

$$\mathcal{E}_L = -\frac{d\Phi}{dt} = -L\frac{dI}{dt}. \tag{10.11}$$

Here we assumed that L does not depend on time.[3] The negative sign in Equation (10.11) indicates that the induced emf opposes the change in the current (Figure 10.2 (a)). As far as the electrical response of a circuit is concerned, the effect of induction is equivalent to a battery inserted so that it resists the change in the current in the inductor (Figure 10.2 (b)). The emf of the equivalent battery can simply be interpreted as the voltage across the inductor at the moment:[4]

$$V_L = -\mathcal{E}_L = +L\frac{dI}{dt}. \tag{10.12}$$

If the current in the coil varies as $I = I_0 \cos \omega t$ in response to applied voltage V, the voltage across the inductor is

$$V_L = -LI_0 \omega \sin \omega t = V_0 \cos\left(\omega t + \frac{\pi}{2}\right), \tag{10.13}$$

which implies that *the voltage across an inductor leads the current by* $\frac{\pi}{2}$. The relationship between I_0 and V_0 is

$$V_0 = (\omega L) I_0. \tag{10.14}$$

Thus an inductor acts like a resistor with resistance ωL, which is called the **inductive reactance**.

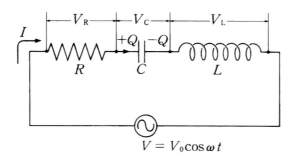

Figure 10.3: Series RLC circuit. The same current $I = I_0 \cos(\omega t - \phi)$ flows in all of the three components.

10.3.2 Series RLC Circuit

Next we consider a series RLC circuit as illustrated in Figure 10.3; a resistor of resistance R [Ω], capacitor of capacitance C [F], and inductor of inductance L [H] connected in series are driven by an AC power supply of angular frequency ω [rad/s] that varies with time as $V = V_0 \cos \omega t$. Letting I be the current in the circuit, the voltage across the inductor V_L, that across the resistor V_R and that across the capacitor V_C are

$$V_L = L\frac{dI}{dt}, \tag{10.15}$$

$$V_R = RI, \tag{10.16}$$

and

$$V_C = \frac{Q}{C}. \tag{10.17}$$

The Kirchhoff's loop rule applied to the circuit yields

$$V = V_L + V_R + V_C = L\frac{dI}{dt} + RI + \frac{Q}{C}. \tag{10.18}$$

Differentiating the both hand sides, we obtain a second-order nonhomogeneous linear equation:

$$L\frac{d^2I}{dt^2} + R\frac{dI}{dt} + \frac{1}{C}I = \frac{dV}{dt}. \tag{10.19}$$

---

[3] This assumption is satisfied if μ does not depend on the magnetic field strength H inside. For many ferromagnetic materials, this is shown to be approximately valid.

[4] Focus on the sign. The voltage *drops* as the battery is traversed from left to right. In the context of a motor, a self-induced emf is known as a *back emf* and often replaced with an equivalent battery as in Figure 10.2 (b) for simplicity.

The general solution of Equation (10.19) is the sum of the general solution of its corresponding homogeneous equation and a particular solution to the nonhomogeneous equation. Since the solution of the homogeneous equation is transient, we are only interested in the particular solution. Equation (10.19) has the same form as the forced oscillation of a spring-mass system and is solved in the same manner. Since the circuit is driven by a generator with an angular frequency of ω, the current I is supposed to oscillate with the identical angular frequency in a steady state, we describe the current as

$$I = I_0 \cos(\omega t - \phi). \tag{10.20}$$

Substituting I and V in Equation (10.19) and simplifying the expression, we get

$$V_0 \sin \omega t = I_0 \left(R \sin(\omega t - \phi) + \left(\omega L - \frac{1}{\omega C}\right) \cos(\omega t - \phi) \right). \tag{10.21}$$

If we express the coefficients of the sine and cosine terms as

$$R = |Z| \cos \alpha, \quad \omega L - \frac{1}{\omega C} = |Z| \sin \alpha, \tag{10.22}$$

where

$$|Z| = \sqrt{R^2 + \left(\omega L - \frac{1}{\omega C}\right)^2}, \quad \alpha = \tan^{-1}\left(\frac{\omega L - \frac{1}{\omega C}}{R}\right). \tag{10.23}$$

Equation (10.21) reduces to

$$V_0 \sin \omega t = |Z| I_0 \sin(\omega t - \phi + \alpha). \tag{10.24}$$

To satisfy Equation (10.24) for arbitrary t, we need

$$V_0 = |Z| I_0, \quad \alpha = \phi. \tag{10.25}$$

The current is expressed explicitly as follows:

$$\begin{aligned} I &= \frac{V_0}{|Z|} \cos(\omega t - \alpha) \\ &= \frac{V_0}{\sqrt{R^2 + \left(\omega L - \frac{1}{\omega C}\right)^2}} \cos\left(\omega t - \tan^{-1}\left(\frac{\omega L - \frac{1}{\omega C}}{R}\right)\right). \end{aligned} \tag{10.26}$$

$|Z|$ is called the **impedance** of the circuit and the phase angle α is conventionally taken as a *delay angle*.

10.3.3 Complex Impedance

Equation (10.19) can be solved more easily with complex numbers. Using Euler's equation $e^{\pm i\omega t} = \cos \omega t \pm i \sin \omega t$, we define V_+ and V_- as

$$V_+ = \frac{1}{2} V_0 e^{i\omega t}, \quad V_- = \frac{1}{2} V_0 e^{-i\omega t}. \tag{10.27}$$

10.3 THEORY

Then the driving voltage is written as

$$V = V_0 \cos \omega t = V_+ + V_-. \tag{10.28}$$

Since Equation (10.19) is a linear equation, its solution can be expressed as $I = I_+ + I_-$: the sum of the solution for the driving voltage V_+ and that for V_-. The solution I_+ for the voltage V_+ is expected to oscillate with an angular frequency of ω, we represent it as

$$I_+ = \frac{1}{2} I_0 e^{i\omega t} \quad (I_0 \text{ is a complex number in general.}) \tag{10.29}$$

We plug it into Equation (10.19) and simplify to obtain

$$V_+ = \left(R + i\omega L + \frac{1}{i\omega C} \right) I_+. \tag{10.30}$$

Here we define Z by

$$Z = R + i\omega L + \frac{1}{i\omega C} = R + i\left(\omega L - \frac{1}{\omega C}\right) = |Z|e^{i\phi}, \tag{10.31}$$

Equation (10.30) simply becomes

$$V_+ = ZI_+. \tag{10.32}$$

This equation has the same form as Ohm's law $V = RI$. The current response I_- to the driving voltage V_- is acquired in the same way. The result is

$$V_- = \left(R - i\omega L - \frac{1}{i\omega C} \right) I_-. \tag{10.33}$$

Letting the complex conjugate of Z be $\overline{Z}$, Equation (10.33) reduces to

$$V_- = \overline{Z} I_-. \tag{10.34}$$

Since $V_- = \overline{V_+}$, the current I is

$$\begin{aligned} I &= I_+ + I_- = \frac{V_+}{Z} + \frac{\overline{V_+}}{\overline{Z}} = \frac{V_+}{Z} + \overline{\left(\frac{V_+}{Z}\right)} = \text{Re}\left(\frac{2V_+}{Z}\right) \\ &= \text{Re}\left(\frac{V_0}{|Z|} e^{i(\omega t - \phi)}\right) = \frac{V_0}{|Z|} \cos(\omega t - \phi). \end{aligned} \tag{10.35}$$

The result is exactly the same as the one obtained in the previous section.

Instead of decomposing V into V_+ and V_-, we can consider the sinusoidal voltage $V = V_0 \cos \omega t$ as the real part of the complex voltage $V = V_0 e^{i\omega t}$. Either way, if you introduce a complex voltage, we can treat an AC circuit just like as a DC circuit. Z is called the *complex impedance* (often we simply call it the impedance). The impedance of the resistor (resistance), that of the inductor (inductive reactance) and that of the capacitor (capacitive reactance) are, respectively,

$$Z_R = R, \tag{10.36}$$

$$Z_L = i\omega L,\tag{10.37}$$

and

$$Z_C = \frac{1}{i\omega C} = -i\frac{1}{\omega C}.\tag{10.38}$$

For a series RLC circuit shown in Figure 10.3, the equivalent impedance is given by the sum of the individual impedance:

$$Z = Z_R + Z_L + Z_C = R + i\left(\omega L - \frac{1}{\omega C}\right).\tag{10.39}$$

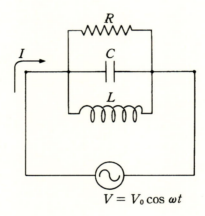

Figure 10.4: Parallel RLC circuit. The same voltage is applied to all of the three components.

The impedance of a parallel RLC circuit illustrated in Figure 10.4 is computed the same way as the resistors connected in parallel in a DC circuit:

$$\frac{1}{Z} = \frac{1}{Z_R} + \frac{1}{Z_L} + \frac{1}{Z_C} = \frac{1}{R} + i\left(\omega C - \frac{1}{\omega L}\right).\tag{10.40}$$

If we write the impedance in the form of

$$Z = R + iX,\tag{10.41}$$

the real part is the resistance and the imaginary part is the reactance.

Figure 10.5 (a) depicts the impedance (Equation (10.41)) in the complex plane. Applying Euler's equation $\cos\phi + i\sin\phi = e^{i\phi}$ to express Z in the polar coordinate $(|Z|, \phi)$, we have

$$Z = \sqrt{R^2 + X^2}\,e^{i\phi}.\tag{10.42}$$

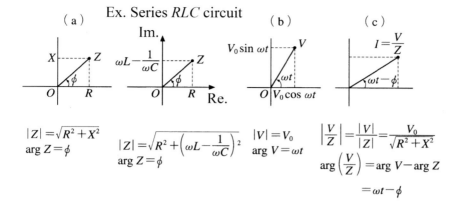

Figure 10.5: Phase angles (phasers) in the complex plane for a series RLC circuit: (a) Impedance Z. (b) Voltage V. (c) Current $I = V/Z$.

The voltage V rotates in the complex plane as shown in Figure 10.5 (b). The complex current I expressed in the polar coordinate is

$$I = \frac{V}{Z} = \frac{V_0 e^{i\omega t}}{\sqrt{R^2 + X^2} e^{i\phi}} = \frac{V_0}{\sqrt{R^2 + X^2}} e^{i(\omega t - \phi)}. \tag{10.43}$$

The actual current is given by its real part

$$I = \text{Re}(I) = I_0 \cos(\omega t - \phi), \tag{10.44}$$

where

$$I_0 = \frac{V_0}{\sqrt{R^2 + X^2}}. \tag{10.45}$$

The power $\overline{P}$ consumed in the circuit is calculated as the average of the consumed energy in one period $T = \dfrac{2\pi}{\omega}$:

$$\overline{P} = \frac{1}{T}\int_0^T IV\,dt = \frac{1}{T}\int_0^T I_0 V_0 \cos(\omega t - \phi)\cos\omega t\,dt = \frac{1}{2}I_0 V_0 \cos\phi. \tag{10.46}$$

Note that the power depends on the phase ϕ. If the impedance of a circuit is a pure imaginary (or equivalently, if the circuit only contains an inductor and a capacitor), there is no power loss in the circuit because $\phi = \pm\dfrac{\pi}{2}$. The effective (rms) current and voltage are defined by $I_e = I_0/\sqrt{2}$ and $V_e = V_0/\sqrt{2}$ respectively. The values measured with ammeters are voltmeters are these effective values.

In a real circuit, the energy is lost in inductors due to resistance in the conducting wires and Eddy currents[5] in the ferromagnetic cores of the coils. These effects are

---

[5] Current loops induced within conductors by varying magnetic fields.

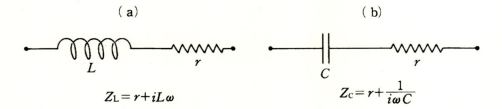

Figure 10.6: (a) Equivalent circuit for an inductor. (b) Equivalent circuit for a capacitor.

described by an internal resistance connected in series with a inductor as depicted in Figure 10.6 (a). The same argument applies to capacitors. Dielectrics such as air ($\varepsilon = 1.0006\varepsilon_0$), ceramic ($\varepsilon = 10^3$–$10^4\varepsilon_0$), plastic ($\varepsilon = 2$–$6\varepsilon_0$) and mica ($\varepsilon = 2$–$8\varepsilon_0$) are inserted between the plates of a capacitor. If their dielectric polarization lags the time varying electric field E, then it causes a phase difference between E and the electric displacement field D, which leads to an energy loss. The energy is also lost due to a leakage current into dielectrics. Taking these losses into account, a real capacitor is treated with an equivalent circuit shown in Figure 10.6 (b).

10.3.4 Resonance in Series RLC Circuit

A pendulum or a tuning fork oscillates with a large amplitude when driven by a specific frequency. This phenomenon is called *resonance*. In a mechanical system, the oscillation is an exchange between the mechanical energy and potential energy, whereas in an electrical circuit it is an exchange between the electric energy and magnetic energy.

The impedance of the series RLC circuit shown in Figure 10.3 is

$$Z = R + iX = R + i\left(\omega L - \frac{1}{\omega C}\right). \tag{10.47}$$

The reactance $X = \omega L - \dfrac{1}{\omega C}$ varies with the angular frequency ω and it completely disappears at a certain value of ω. Such frequency is called the **resonant frequency**, and it is given by

$$\omega_0 = \frac{1}{\sqrt{LC}}. \tag{10.48}$$

Since the impedance $|Z| = \sqrt{R^2 + X^2}$ takes a minimum value at the resonant frequency, the current

$$|I| = I_0 = \left|\frac{V}{Z}\right| = \frac{|V|}{|Z|} = \frac{V_0}{\sqrt{R^2 + X^2}} \tag{10.49}$$

takes a maximum value. This is termed the series resonance.

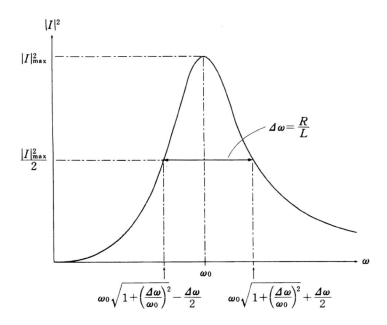

Figure 10.7: Resonance curve for series RLC circuit. $|I|^2$ (proportional to the power) is plotted against the angular frequency of the driving voltage. The curve peaks at the resonant frequency ω_0. Half-width $\Delta\omega$ is the width the curve at the half of the maximum value.

Figure 10.7 is a plot of $|I|^2$ vs. ω graph obtained from Equation (10.49), in which the maximum value of $|I|^2$ is $|I|^2_{\max} = \dfrac{|V_0|^2}{R^2}$. The values of ω where $|I|^2$ is the half of $|I|^2_{\max}$ are

$$\omega_1 = \sqrt{\omega_0^2 + \left(\frac{R}{2L}\right)^2} - \frac{R}{2L} \tag{10.50}$$

$$\omega_2 = \sqrt{\omega_0^2 + \left(\frac{R}{2L}\right)^2} + \frac{R}{2L}. \tag{10.51}$$

$\Delta\omega = \omega_2 - \omega_1$ is called the **half-width**.[6] The sharpness of the curve is evaluated by the **Q factor** (quality factor). It is defined by

$$Q \equiv \frac{\omega_0}{\omega_2 - \omega_1}. \tag{10.52}$$

The resonance curve is sharper if it has a larger value of Q factor. For the series

---

[6] Exactly speaking, $\Delta\omega$ is termed the full width at half maximum (FWHM). The half of the FWHM, $\dfrac{\Delta\omega}{2}$, is known as the half-width at half maximum (HWHM).

RLC circuit, Q factor is

$$Q = \frac{\omega_0 L}{R} = \frac{\frac{1}{\omega_0 C}}{R} = \frac{1}{R}\sqrt{\frac{L}{C}}. \qquad (10.53)$$

Thus the curve is sharper if the resistance in the circuit is smaller. At the resonant frequency, the voltage across the capacitor or inductor is Q times as large as V_0.

The magnetic energy E_L stored in the inductor and the electric energy E_C stored in the capacitor are, respectively,

$$E_L = \frac{1}{2}LI^2 = \frac{1}{2}L\left(\frac{V_0}{R}\cos\omega_0 t\right)^2 = \frac{LV_0^2}{2R^2}\cos^2\omega_0 t \qquad (10.54)$$

$$E_C = \frac{1}{2}CV_C^2 = \frac{1}{2}C\left(\frac{V_0}{\omega_0 CR}\sin\omega_0 t\right)^2 = \frac{LV_0^2}{2R^2}\sin^2\omega_0 t. \qquad (10.55)$$

We can see that the energies are exchanged between the inductor and capacitor, and their sum is a constant:

$$E_L + E_C = \frac{LV_0^2}{2R^2}. \qquad (10.56)$$

10.3.5 Resonance in Parallel LC Circuit

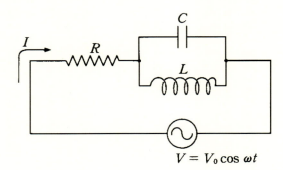

Figure 10.8: Parallel LC circuit. I_L and I_C counteract each other. I_R vanishes and V_L and V_C are maximized at ω_0. This configuration works as a band-pass filter in a filter circuit.

The impedance of the parallel LC circuit illustrated in Figure 10.8 is

$$Z = R + i\frac{1}{\frac{1}{\omega L} - \omega C}. \qquad (10.57)$$

Since the inductorand capacitor are in parallel in this circuit, the voltages across the two components are the same. For this reason, the phase difference between the current in the inductor I_L and that in the capacitor I_C is π, and they offset each other. At the resonant frequency $\omega_0 = \dfrac{1}{\sqrt{LC}}$, I_L and I_C completely cancel, and the current stops in the circuit. There the impedance diverges, and V_L and V_C take the maximum value V (the driving voltage).[7]

10.4 Apparatus

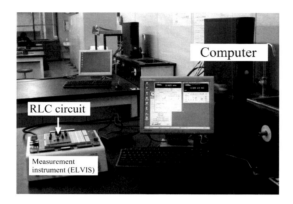

Figure 10.9: Overview of the experimental setup.

10.4.1 ELVIS

Figure 10.9 shows an overview of the equipment used in this laboratory. It consists of an RLC circuit embedded in the breadboard on top of the measurement instrument (ELVIS®[8]) by National Instruments). The instrument is controlled by the NI ELVIS software installed in the computer and works as various types of measuring devices and analyzers. A function generator is also built in the ELVIS to supply several different waveforms of AC voltage over a wide range of frequencies.

10.4.2 RLC Circuit

The RLC circuit mounted on the ELVIS carries several switches on it, which enable us to change its configurations and the values of the circuit components. The series RLC circuit used in this laboratory is illustrated in Figure 10.10. The AC source is the function generator; the inductors consist of conducting wires wound around ferrite cores.[9] The permeability μ of ferromagnetic materials such as ferrite is

---

[7] In practice, the impedance is finite and a small current still remains at ω_0 due to the internal resistances of the inductor and the capacitor.

[8] Acronym for Educational Laboratory Virtual Instrumentation Suite.

[9] Ferrite was is a ferromagnetic ceramic material first synthesized by Yogoro Kato and Takeshi Takei at the Tokyo Institute of Technology in 1930.

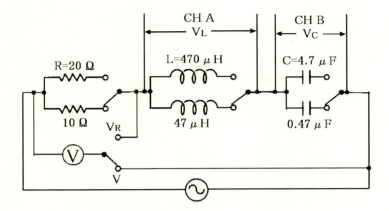

Figure 10.10: A circuit diagram of the RLC circuit used in this experiment.

very large compared to that of free space $\mu_0 = 4\pi \times 10^{-7}$ H/m ($\mu/\mu_0 = 10$–10^5). It is impossible to achieve a practical value of inductance without ferromagnetic materials.

10.5 Procedure

10.5.1 Setup

1. Launching ELVIS

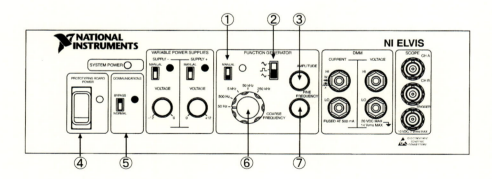

Figure 10.11: Front panel of the ELVIS: ① Manual control switch. ② Wave form selector. ③ Amplitude control. ④ Power switch. ⑤ Normal/Bypass switch. ⑥ Coarse frequency control. ⑦ Fine frequency control.

10.5 PROCEDURE

Plug the power cable of the ELVIS and turn on the two power switches of the ELVIS: first turn on the switch on its back and then the one on the front panel ④ (Figure 10.11). Once confirming the three lamps on top of the ELVIS are on, boot the computer, log in, and click NI ELVIS icon to start the program. (Although an error message sometimes pops up, you can ignore it and just press Enter.) A menu box (Figure 10.12) will be displayed on the screen.

2. Setup of the circuit and function generator

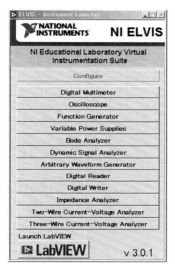

Figure 10.12: Menu box. Digital Multimeter, Oscilloscope and Function Generator will be used.

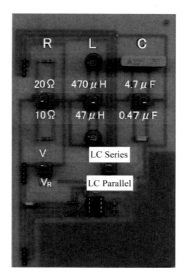

Figure 10.13: RLC circuit board. The types of the circuits, the connection of the voltmeter, and the values of the circuit components are altered by selector switches.

(a) Set the LC Series/Parallel Switch on the circuit board to Series and the resistor, inductor and capacitor selectors to $R{=}10(\Omega)$, $L{=}47(\mu H)$ and $C{=}0.47(\mu F)$ respectively.

(b) On the front panel of the ELVIS, turn on the manual control switch ① and select sine wave ($\sim$) ② to supply a sinusoidal voltage. This setting allows us to control the amplitude and frequency of the applied voltage with the control knobs on the panel.

3. Adjustment of amplitude and frequency From the application list in the menu box, choose Digital Multimeter and Function Generator. We will use the former to measure the amplitude of the applied voltage or voltage across the resistor and the latter to vary its frequency.

(a) Set V/V_R switch on the circuit board to V to examine the applied voltage.

114 CHAPTER 10 AC CIRCUITS AND RESONANCE

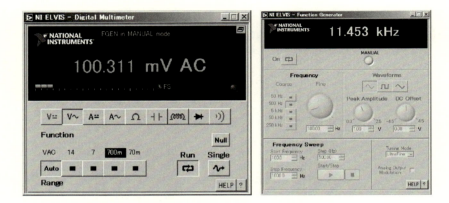

Figure 10.14: Application window of Digital Multimeter (left) and that of Function Generator (right).

(b) Click $V\sim$ in the Digital Multimeter dialog box to see the amplitude (effective value) of the applied AC voltage. Turn the amplitude control knob ③ on the panel of the ELVIS to set the amplitude to be 100 mV. We will keep this amplitude throughout the experiment.

(c) Turn the coarse frequency control ⑥ and the fine frequency control ⑦ on the ELVIS panel to set the frequency about 30 kHz.

10.5.2 Phases of V_R, V_L and V_C

We will investigate the phase differences among the voltages across the resistor V_R, inductor V_L and capacitor V_C in the series RLC circuit.

1. Close Digital Multimeter first and click Oscilloscope to start the application. (We cannot use Digital Multimeter and Oscilloscope at the same time, and you will get an error message if you launch Oscilloscope while Multimeter is still open.)

2. In the Oscilloscope dialog box, confirm the Source in the Trigger section is SYNC_OUT.

3. The signals displayed on the left side of the box are selected by Source of CHANNEL A and that of CHANNEL B:

	Source	Displayed signal
CHANNEL A	BNC/Board CH A	Voltage across inductor
	DMM Voltage	Source voltage or voltage across resistor*
CHANNEL B	BNC/Board CH B	Voltage across capacitor
	DMM Voltage	Source voltage or voltage across resistor*

*Selected by V/V_R switch.

4. Adjust the vertical and horizontal scales by changing VERTICAL and TIME-BASE controls.

5. Sketch the waveforms of the applied voltage V, the voltages across the resistor V_R, capacitor V_C and inductor V_L at 30 kHz to verify that their phase differences agree with theory. Switch the V/V_R selector back and force to examine a small phase difference between V and V_R.

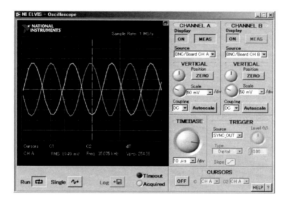

Figure 10.15: Oscilloscope window. VERTICAL and TIMEBASE controls will be used to adjust the axis scales.

10.5.3 Resonance Curve for Series RLC Circuit

In this part of the experiment, we will observe how the current I_e in a series RLC circuit changes with the driving frequency f. The value of the current will be computed as $I_e = V_{eR}/R$, where V_{eR} is the effective voltage across the resistor.

1. Set the values of the resistor, inductor and capacitor. Choose one of the combinations described in the following table.

Combination	R(Ω)	L(μH)	C(μF)
A	10	47	0.47
B	10	47	4.7
C	10	470	0.47
D	20	47	0.47

2. Flip V/V_R switch on the circuit board to V_R to measure the voltage across the resistor.

3. Close Oscilloscope and open Digital multimeter. Click $V \sim$ to display V_{eR}.

4. Launch Function Generator. The frequency of the voltage across the resistor will be exhibited on the display; note that this is identical to the frequency of the source voltage.

5. Turn the COURSE FREQUENCY control ⑥ and FINE FREQUENCY control ⑦ on the front panel of ELVIS to change the frequency, and read the value of V_{eR}. Calculate $I_e^2 = (V_{eR}/R)^2$ and plot a I_e^2 vs. f graph. First vary the frequency coarsely to get the overall shape of the graph, then examine the behavior around the resonant frequency and half-maxima more closely. It is more efficient to compute I_e^2 and plot a data point each time you measure the value of V_{eR} than to plot a graph after finishing all the measurements.

6. Determine the resonant frequency and half-width from your graph, and compute Q factor using Equation (10.52). Compare the result with the theoretical value of the half-width, which is calculated from Equation (10.53).

7. (Optional) Conduct the measurement of the resonance curve for another combination in the table above.

10.5.4 Frequency Dependencies of V_L and V_C

Explore the frequency dependence of the voltage across the inductor V_L and that across the capacitor V_C. Launch Function Generator and Oscilloscope, and observe the waveforms at various frequencies. Verify that the two voltages cancel at the resonance frequency.

10.5.5 Resonance Curve for Parallel LC Circuit

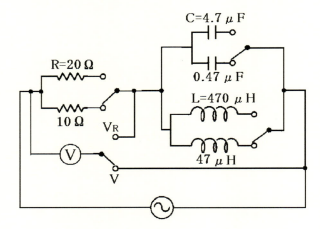

Figure 10.16: Parallel LC circuit. Set V/V_R switch to V_R to plot a resonance curve.

Set LC Series/LC Parallel switch on the circuit board to LC Parallel. The circuit diagram of this configuration is depicted in Figure 10.16. Using $R = 10 \ \Omega$, $L = 47 \ \mu$H and $C = 0.47 \ \mu$F, measure the frequency dependence of V_R the same way as you did for a series RLC circuit and plot a resonance curve (I_e^2 vs. f) for the parallel LC circuit.

10.6 Comprehension Questions

1. Prove that the Q factor for series RLC circuits is expressed in terms of the resonance angular frequency ω_0 as

$$Q = \omega_0 \tau_e, \qquad (10.58)$$

where τ_e is the time constant for the total electromagnetic energy in undriven RLC circuits (time required for the energy to decrease by a factor of $1/e$).

2. Discuss the effect of the internal resistance of a capacitor and that of an inductor in a series RLC circuit. How do they affect the values of its resonant frequency, half-width and Q factor?

3. Derive the expression for the complex impedance of parallel LC circuits (Equation (10.8)).

Chapter 11

Frequency Dependence of Amplifier

11.1 Introduction

A filter is a circuit component that allows signals within a specific range of frequencies to pass and blocks those outside the range, and it is crucial to many electronic circuit systems. Communication and audio systems, for example, utilize filters to reduce noise and achieve best sound quality. Physics and engineering experiments often require them to detect signals hidden in background noises. In a digital circuit system, filters are indispensable to avoid a phenomenon called aliasing.[1] Today we will explore the frequency dependence of a **low-pass filter** (a filter that attenuates high frequency signals) and that of a **high-pass filter** (a filter that attenuates low frequency signals) to learn about the basics of filter circuits.

11.2 Objective

1. Using sinusoidal waves ranging 10 Hz–1 MHz, we will measure the frequency dependence of an RC-coupled amplifier in order to study the characteristics and mechanisms of a high-pass filter and low-pass filter used in the amplifier.

2. We will familiarize ourselves to oscilloscopes and signal generators through the experiment.

3. The physical properties of diodes and transistors will be clarified, and their rudimentary functions as rectifiers and amplifiers will be understood.

---

[1] The misidentification of a signal due to a discrete sampling is called aliasing; it can be minimized by suppressing high frequency signals.

11.3 Theory

11.3.1 Amplification of *RC*-Coupled Amplifier

An RC-coupled amplifier is a multistage amplifier in which its stages are connected with resistors and capacitors. Figure 11.1 shows a schematic of the RC-coupled amplifier used in this laboratory;[2] it consists of a C_H-R_H high-pass filter, the first negative feedback amplifier, a R_L-C_L low-pass filter, and the second negative feedback amplifier. The frequency dependence of an RC-coupled amplifier to sinusoidal input signals is depicted in Figure 11.2. The amplification drops for frequencies lower than f_H because the reactance of C_H in the high-pass filter gets larger and the input signal into the first amplifier diminishes. On the other hand, the drop of the amplification for frequencies higher than f_L is caused by a decrease in the capacitive reactance C_L and which attenuates the input signal into the second amplifier.

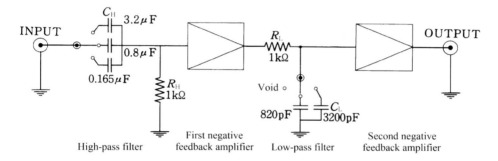

Figure 11.1: A block diagram of the RC-coupled amplifier used in this experiment. Several values of C_H and C_L can be selected to regulate the output signal.

A *negative feedback amplifier* is an amplifier in which the negative of a fraction of the output signal is fed back to the input signal. Negative feedback stabilizes the amplifier because the output change due to an external factor is counteracted by the feedback. The amplification of transistors in the negative feedback amplifiers used in the laboratory decreases at high frequencies. However, their cutoff frequencies are sufficiently high (above 100 MHz), and we can assume that the amplifications of the first and second amplifiers in the RC-coupled circuit are independent of frequencies.

Now let's consider the frequency dependence of the output voltage when a sinusoidal voltage of frequency f, $\tilde{V}_{in} = V_{in} \sin \omega t$ (where $\omega = 2\pi f$ is the angular frequency) is applied to an RC-coupled amplifier. Figure 11.1 is represented by an equivalent circuit shown in Figure 11.3. Note that the configuration of a high-pass filter and that of a low-pass filter are the same, a resistor and a capacitor connected in a series. They merely differ in that the output voltage of a high-pass filter is taken from its resistor R_H, while the output of a low-pass filter is picked up from its capacitor C_L. The voltage across R_H, which makes up an input voltage into the first amplifier, oscillates sinusoidally with the same frequency as the applied voltage.

---

[2] Its complete circuit diagram is illustrated in Figure 11.9.

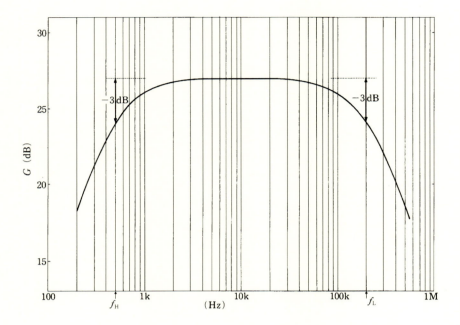

Figure 11.2: A sample graph of power gain *vs.* frequency for an *RC*-coupled amplifier. The vertical axis is the gain (output/input) in dB, and the horizontal axis is the frequency on a logarithmic scale. The graph shows a flat gain over a range of frequencies approximately from 1 kHz to 100 kHz. The frequencies at which gain in dB falls from its maximum value by 3 dB are called *cutoff frequencies*.

However, their phases are different by ϕ_H because of the capacitor C_H connected in series with the resistor (refer to Comprehension Question 1):

$$\tilde{V}_{R_H} = \frac{V_{\text{in}}}{\sqrt{1+\left(\frac{1}{R_H C_H \omega}\right)^2}} \sin(\omega t + \phi_H) \tag{11.1}$$

$$\tan \phi_H = \frac{1}{R_H C_H \omega}. \tag{11.2}$$

This voltage is amplified by the first negative feedback amplifier. Denoting the voltage gain (a.k.a. voltage amplification factor, ratio of the output voltage to the input voltage) of the amplifier as A_1, and its phase shift as ϕ_1, the output voltage $\tilde{V}_{o'}$ is

$$\tilde{V}_{o'} = \frac{V_{\text{in}}}{\sqrt{1+\left(\frac{1}{R_H C_H \omega}\right)^2}} A_1 \sin(\omega t + \phi_H + \phi_1), \tag{11.3}$$

where ϕ_1 depends on the internal structure of the amplifier. Next, the output voltage of the low-pass filter, i.e., voltage across the capacitor C_L again acquires an extra

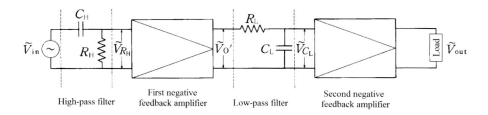

Figure 11.3: A circuit diagram equivalent to the RC-coupled amplifier used in this experiment. The high-pass filter and low-pass filters are both equivalent to series RC circuits; the only difference is the order of the connections.

amount of phase shift ϕ_2 (Comprehension Question 1):

$$\tilde{V}_{C_L} = \frac{V_{in}}{\sqrt{1+\left(\frac{1}{R_H C_H \omega}\right)^2}} A_1 \frac{1}{\sqrt{1+(R_L C_L \omega)^2}} \sin(\omega t + \phi_H + \phi_1 + \phi_L)$$

$$\tan\phi_L = -R_L C_L \omega. \tag{11.4}$$

Lastly, this voltage is amplified by the second negative feedback amplifier and is taken as the final output. Letting A_2 and ϕ_2 be the voltage gain of the amplifier and its phase shift respectively, the final output voltage is

$$\tilde{V}_{out} = \frac{V_{in}}{\sqrt{1+\left(\frac{1}{R_H C_H \omega}\right)^2}} A_1 \frac{1}{\sqrt{1+(R_L C_L \omega)^2}} A_2 \sin(\omega t + \phi_H + \phi_1 + \phi_L + \phi_2)$$

$$= V_{out} \sin(\omega t + \phi_{out}). \tag{11.5}$$

The output voltage of the entire amplifier is sinusoidal with the same frequency as the input; its amplitude is augmented and its phase is altered. We shall not deal with the phase shift in this experiment, so let's focus on the amplitude. The voltage gain is

$$\frac{V_{out}}{V_{in}} = A_1 A_2 \frac{1}{\sqrt{1+\left(\frac{1}{R_H C_H \omega}\right)^2}} \frac{1}{\sqrt{1+(R_L C_L \omega)^2}}. \tag{11.6}$$

The gain of an amplifier normally takes a large value. Therefore, it is customary to express it in terms of its common logarithm. The power gain, or the power ratio P_{out}/P_{in} in decibel is defined by[3]

$$G \text{ [dB]} = 10 \log_{10} \frac{P_{out}}{P_{in}}. \tag{11.7}$$

---

[3] A decibel is the unit equal to 1/10 of a bell, which is defined by $\log_{10} P_{out}/P_{in}$. The unit of decibel is originally employed to describe the power loss of a telephone line, and named after Alexander Graham Bell, an inventor of the telephone.

Since the power is proportional to the square of the voltage, the power gain in decibel is expressed in terms of the voltage gain as

$$G \text{ [dB]} = 10 \log_{10} \left(\frac{V_{\text{out}}}{V_{\text{in}}}\right)^2 = 20 \log_{10} \frac{V_{\text{out}}}{V_{\text{in}}}. \tag{11.8}$$

Substituting Equation (11.6) into Equation (11.8), we obtain the frequency dependence of the gain for the *RC*-coupled amplifier:

$$G \text{ [dB]} = 20 \log_{10} A_1 A_2 + 20 \log_{10} \frac{1}{\sqrt{1 + \left(\frac{1}{R_{\text{H}} C_{\text{H}} \omega}\right)^2}} + 20 \log_{10} \frac{1}{\sqrt{1 + (R_{\text{L}} C_{\text{L}} \omega)^2}}. \tag{11.9}$$

The first term in Equation (11.9) represents the overall gain of the two feedback amplifiers. For the amplifier used in this laboratory, $A_1 A_2$ is approximately 22, or $20 \log_{10} A_1 A_2 \sim 27$ dB, and it does not depend on ω. The second and third terms are the gains of the two filters. Note that their component values satisfy $R_{\text{L}} C_{\text{L}} \ll R_{\text{H}} C_{\text{H}}$. If a sinusoidal signal with angular frequency $\omega < 1/R_{\text{H}} C_{\text{H}}$ is applied to the amplifier, the second term takes a negative value and the third term is essentially zero, whereas for input frequency $\omega > 1/R_{\text{L}} C_{\text{L}}$ the second term is zero and the third term is negative. This signifies that high-pass filters pass signals with high frequencies and attenuate low frequencies, while low-pass filters pass low frequency signals and suppress high frequencies.[4]

The frequencies at which the output power is reduced to the half of the maximum, or the output voltage decreases by a factor of $\sqrt{2}$ ($V_{\text{out}}/V_{\text{in}} \simeq A_1 A_2 / \sqrt{2}$) define lower cutoff frequency f_{H} ($= \omega_{\text{H}}/2\pi$) and upper cutoff frequency f_{L} ($= \omega_{\text{L}}/2\pi$). These correspond to the frequencies at which the power gain in dB becomes -3 dB from the maximum gain since $10 \log_{10}(1/2) = 20 \log_{10}(1/\sqrt{2}) \approx -3$ dB. The frequency range between f_{H} and f_{L} is called the *passband* and the regions outside of them are called the *stopband*. From Equation (11.9), f_{H} and f_{L} are found to be

$$f_{\text{H}} = \frac{1}{2\pi R_{\text{H}} C_{\text{H}}}, \qquad f_{\text{L}} = \frac{1}{2\pi R_{\text{L}} C_{\text{L}}}. \tag{11.10}$$

For example, if we assume $C_{\text{H}}=0.32$ μF and $R_{\text{H}}=1$ kΩ, then we obtain $f_{\text{H}}=497$ Hz. If $C_{\text{L}}=820$ pF and $R_{\text{L}}=1$ kΩ, we get $f_{\text{L}}=194$ kHz. Figure 11.2 shows the frequency dependence of the gain expressed by Equation (11.9) with these sample values and $20 \log A_1 A_2 = 27$ dB.

11.3.2 Principles of Oscilloscope

An oscilloscope is a device for observing voltage signals. In this section we will discuss the mechanism of a CRT (cathode ray tube) oscilloscope. As depicted in Figure 11.4, it consists of an electron gun to emit and focus an electron beam, deflection plates to regulate the direction of the beam, and a fluorescent screen that

---

[4] Thus high-pass filters and low-pass filters are also called *low-cut filters* and *high-cut filters* respectively.

11.3 THEORY

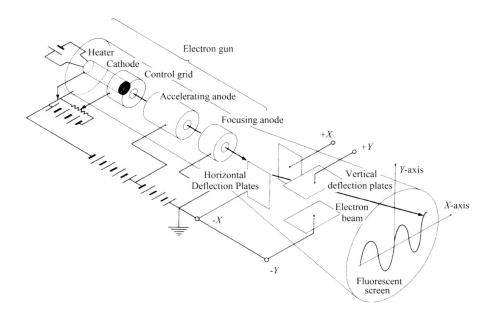

Figure 11.4: Schematic of a CRT oscilloscope. A beam of electrons is emitted and accelerated in the electron gun, then it is bent by two sets of the deflection plates before hitting the fluorescent screen.

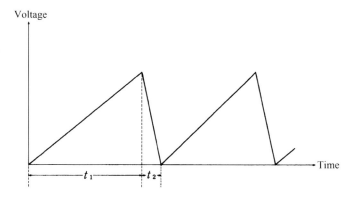

Figure 11.5: Sawtooth sweep: t_1 is called the sweep time and t_2 is the retrace time. A bright spot on the screen is swept to the right at a constant speed during t_1, then comes back to the original position during t_2.

produces a bright spot when hit by an electron. When the cathode in is heated, elections are ejected from it. After the electrons are regulated by the control grid, they are accelerated and focused by the two anodes. If a periodic voltage is applied to the horizontal or vertical deflection plates, the beam oscillates in the horizontal or vertical direction respectively.

To observe the waveform of a time-varying voltage, the voltage is applied to the vertical deflection plates and a periodic saw-tooth voltage called *sweep* to the horizontal plates. The saw-tooth voltage is proportional to time as shown in Figure 11.5 to sweep the bright spot uniformly from left to right for a time interval called the sweep time. Then the spot returns to its original spot during a short time interval called the retrace time. The control grid is arranged so that the trajectory of the bright spot is not shown on the screen during the retrace time. Suppose a

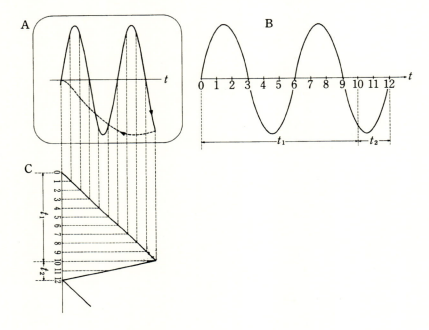

Figure 11.6: A: Waveform displayed on the fluorescent screen, the dashed line represents the motion of the bright spot during the retrace time. (This dashed line can be removed by applying a negative voltage to the control grid during the retrace time.) B: Sinusoidal wave applied to the vertical deflection plates. C: Saw-tooth sweep voltage applied to the horizontal deflection plates.

periodic voltage of frequency f_y is applied to the vertical deflection plates. If the ratio of f_y to the frequency of the sweep voltage f_x is an integer ratio, the waveform of the periodic voltage gets stationary. For example, if f_x has a frequency equal to f_y/n (n is an integer), a stationary waveform is observed on the screen. Figure 11.6 represents the case of $n = 2$. The operation to match f_x to f_y/n is called synchronization. If they are not synchronized, the signal drifts horizontally.

It is not easy to produce a synchronized sweep from a generator independent from the signal of interest, and sweep waves are normally *triggered* by the signal. As shown in Figure 11.7, if a cycle of a saw-tooth sweep is generated as the input voltage reaches a designated value (trigger level), the input signal and sweep are

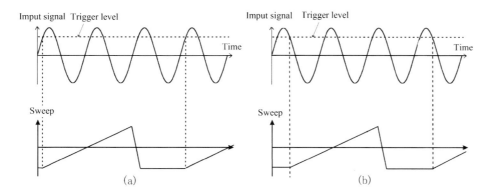

Figure 11.7: Two types of triggering. Trigger points are determined by both the trigger level and the slope of the signal. (a) Positive slope trigger. The trigger is set off only when signal voltage originally lower than the trigger level exceeds the level. (b) Negative slope trigger. The falling portion of the signal needs to hit the trigger level.

synchronized. With this trigger system we can observe waveforms not only for periodic waves, but also irregular waves and pulse waves. There are two types of triggers: a positive trigger that generates a cycle of sweep when input signal reaches a designated trigger level while increasing, and a negative trigger that triggers a sweep when a signal passes a trigger level while decreasing. If a trigger level is set outside of the maximum value of a signal voltage, sweeps are not produced and a stationary waveform is not displayed on the screen.

If, instead of applying a sweep, a sinusoidal wave $X = V_x \cos(2\pi f_x t + \phi_x)$ is applied in the horizontal direction to observe a sinusoidal input voltage $Y = V_y \cos(2\pi f_y t + \phi_y)$, the locus of the bright spot (X, Y) constructs a *Lissajous figure*.[5] If the ratio f_x/f_y is an integer, the figure is fixed on the display. Also, the shape of a Lissajous figure varies depending on the relationship between ϕ_x and ϕ_y as shown in Figure 11.8. Figure 11.8 represents the case of $V_x = V_y$ and several Lissajous curves are illustrated for different values of $\Delta = \phi_y - (f_x/f_y)\phi_x$. Lissajous figures are used to investigate the relationships of two different sinusoidal waves. This type of oscilloscope is called X-Y oscilloscope.

11.4 Apparatus

11.4.1 Signal Generator

A signal generator is an electronic device that produces periodic signals of various frequencies, amplitudes and shapes. The generator used in this laboratory generates sinusoidal or rectangular waves at frequencies 10 Hz–1 MHz.

---

[5] Patterns obtained by superimposing two harmonic vibrations along perpendicular axes. These curves are examined by French mathematician Jules-Antoine Lissajous around 1857.

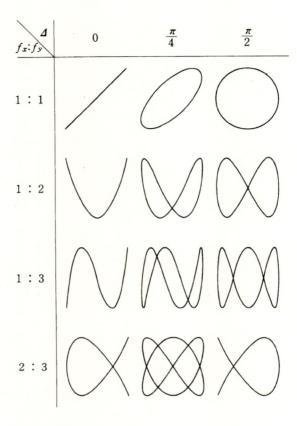

Figure 11.8: Lissajous figures for $X = V_x \cos(2\pi f_x t + \phi_x)$ and $Y = V_y \cos(2\pi f_y t + \phi_y)$. The figures depend on the ratio $f_x : f_y$ and Δ.

11.4.2 Amplifier

Figure 11.9[6] provides the complete circuit diagram of the multistage amplifier used in this laboratory. Three values of the capacitors in the high-pass filter (C_H: 3.2 μF, 0.8 μF, 0.165 μF) and those in the low-pass filters (C_L: 3200 pF, 820 pF, Out) can be selected. The resistors in the two filters have the same fixed value: $R_H = R_L = 1$ kΩ. The characteristics of the amplifier are given in the following table.

11.4.3 Oscilloscope

Figure 11.10 illustrates the front panel of the oscilloscope used in this experiment. (HITACHI, Model V-252) The following is the functions of the controls:

Power

---

[6] The fundamental mechanisms of transistors are accounted for in 11.A Diodes and Transistors.

11.4 APPARATUS

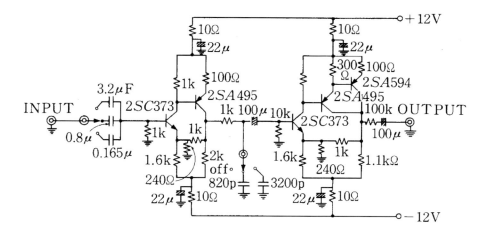

Figure 11.9: Complete circuit diagram of the RC-coupled amplifier. The negative feedback amplifiers consist of multiple transistors.

Table 1: Properties of the multistage amplifier.

Input polarity	Bipolar
Input impedance	1 kΩ
Gain	Each of the negative feedback amplifier: $\sim$ 5 dB
	Total gain: $\sim$ 27 dB
Linearity	Limit of output linearity against input: $\sim \pm 6$ V
Lower cutoff frequency (-3 dB)	50 Hz (3.2 μF), 200 Hz (0.8 μF), 1 kHz (0.165 μF)
Higher cutoff frequency (-3 dB)	50 kHz (3200 pF), 200 kHz (820 pF), 3.4 MHz (Out)

① Power Indicator: Lights when the oscilloscope is on.

② POWER Button: The oscilloscope is ON when the button is pushed in and OFF when it juts out.

Trace Controls

③ TRACE ROTATION: Adjust this knob if the 0 V line of an input voltage is tilted with respect to the X-axis due to an external factor such as the geomagnetic field.

④ INTENSITY: Adjusts the brightness of a bright spot on the display. Set it to zero (turn counterclockwise to the end) before switching on the oscilloscope.

⑤ FOCUS: Change the voltage of the focusing anode to change the sharpness of the waveform.

Horizontal Controls

128   CHAPTER 11 FREQUENCY DEPENDENCE OF AMPLIFIER

⑥ TIME/DIV: Designates the sweep time scale at 19 different values from 0.2 μs/DIV to 0.2 s/DIV. If it is set at X-Y, it works as an X-Y oscilloscope with CH1 as the X-axis and CH2 as the Y-axis.

⑦ SWP VAR: Fine-controls the sweep time scale. Set it to the CAL position (turn it clockwise to the end) to calibrate the division to actual time interval.

⑧ POSITION: Moves the signal horizontally.

Vertical Controls

⑨ MODE: Selects the signal displayed on the screen.

  CH1: The signal of CH1 is displayed.
  CH2: The signal of CH2 is displayed.
  ALT: The signal of CH1 and that of CH2 are displayed alternately.
  ADD: The sum of the CH1 signal and CH2 signal is displayed.

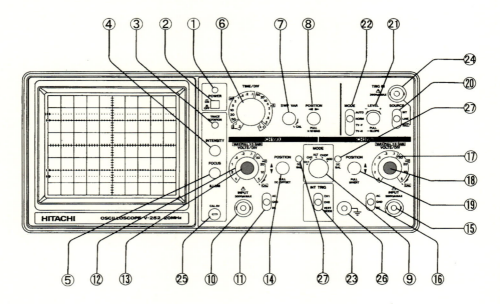

Figure 11.10: Front panel of the oscilloscope. ①–②: Power. ③–⑤: Trace controls. ⑥–⑧: Horizontal controls. ⑨–⑲: Vertical controls. (⑩–⑭: CH1. ⑮–⑲: CH2.) ⑳–㉔: Synchronization. ㉕: Calibration. ㉖: Ground.

CH1

⑩ INPUT: The input terminal for CH1 (or for the X-axis in the X-Y mode).

⑪ AC-GND-CD: Selects connections between the CH1 input signal and the vertical amplifier built in the oscilloscope.

11.4 APPARATUS

   AC: Connected through a capacitor. The DC component of the input signal will be removed.

   GND: The input signal is grounded. Used to check the zero level.

   DC: Connected directly. The input signal is displayed including its DC components.

⑫ VOLTS/DIV (outside knob of the double control): Adjusts the vertical scale for CH1. If the VAR switch ⑬ is at the CAL position, each vertical division coincides with the voltage specified.

⑬ VAR (inside gray knob of the double control): Fine-controls the sensitivity in the vertical scale of CH1. Set it to the CAL position (turn clockwise to the end) to have the vertical scale show the actual voltage designated by ⑫.

⑭ POSITION: Moves the CH 1 signal in the vertical direction.

CH2

⑮INPUT: The input terminal for CH2 (or for the Y-axis in the X-Y mode).

⑯AC-GND-DC: Selects connections between the CH2 input signal and the vertical amplifier built in the oscilloscope.

   AC: Connected through a capacitor. The DC component of the input signal will be removed.

   GND: The input signal is grounded. Used to check the zero level.

   DC: Connected directly. The input signal is displayed including its DC components.

⑰VOLTS/DIV (outside knob of the double control): Adjusts the vertical scale for CH2. If the VAR switch ⑱ is at the CAL position, each vertical division coincides with the voltage specified.

⑱VAR (inside gray knob of the double control): Fine-controls the sensitivity in the vertical scale of CH2. Set it to the CAL position (turn clockwise to the end) to have the vertical scale show the actual voltage designated by ⑰.

⑲POSITON: Moves the CH 2 signal in the vertical direction.

Synchronization

⑳ SOURCE: Selects the source for synchronization.

   INT: Synchronizes with CH1 or CH2 signal (selected by ㉓).

   LINE: Used to monitor a signal synchronized with the frequency of the outlet voltage.

   EXT: Uses an external source (connected to the TRIG IN terminal ㉔) for synchronization.

㉑ LEVEL: Adjusts the trigger level.

130 CHAPTER 11 FREQUENCY DEPENDENCE OF AMPLIFIER

㉒ MODE: Select the trigger mode.

> AUTO: Synchronization is conducted automatically.
>
> NORM: Executes synchronization only when a input signal is detected.

㉓ INT TRIG: Selects the signal for synchronization.

> CH1: Synchronizes with the CH1 signal.
>
> CH2: Synchronizes with the CH2 signal.
>
> VERT MODE: When ⑨ is set to ALT, synchronized with the CH1 signal and CH2 signal alternately.

㉔ TRIG IN: A terminal to use an external signal for synchronization.

Calibration

㉕ CAL: Output terminal of a rectangular wave (0.5 V ± 3 % at 1 kHz). Used to calibrate the vertical scale.

Others

㉖ GND: Grounding terminal.

11.5 Procedure

11.5.1 Setup

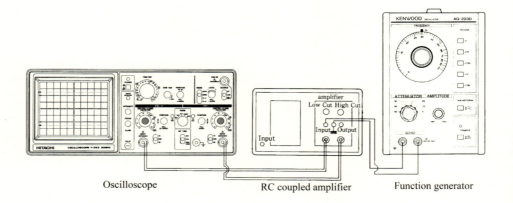

Figure 11.11: Connection of the function generator, RC-coupled amplifier and oscilloscope.

1. Connect the signal generator, RC-coupled amplifier and oscilloscope as illustrated in Figure 11.11.

11.5 PROCEDURE

(a) Connect the OUTPUT terminals of the signal generator to the INPUT terminals (banana jacks) of the amplifier with a pair banana cables. (Make sure to align their polarities: Wire the grounded terminal of the OUTPUT to the grounded terminal of the INPUT.)

(b) The input signal of the amplifier is taken out of its INPUT terminal (BNC connector). Connect it to CH1 INPUT terminal of the oscilloscope ⑩ with a coaxial cable. The input signal will be observed using CH1 of the oscilloscope.

(c) The output signal of the amplifier is obtained from its OUTPUT terminal (BNC connector). Connect it to CH2 INPUT terminal of the oscilloscope ⑮ with a coaxial cable so that the output signal is observed with CH2 of the oscilloscope.

2. Setup the signal generated from the signal generator.

  (a) The waveform of the signal is selected with the WAVEFORM button. Choose sinusoidal wave ($\sim$).

  (b) The frequency of the signal is adjusted with the FREQUENCY dial and RANGE buttons. First turn the FREQUENCY dial to 10 and choose $\times 100$ RANGE button to set the frequency to 10×100 Hz = 1 kHz.

  (c) The amplitude of the signal is regulated with the AMPLITUDE knob and the ATTENUATOR switch; the ATTENUATOR switch coarsely varies the amplitude, while the AMPLITUDE knob is used for fine adjustments. In this experiment, we fix the ATTENUATOR switch to -20 dB and adjust the amplitude only with the AMPLITUDE knob. The input voltage can be adjusted in a range 0.1–0.2 V with this setting.

3. Setup the oscilloscope to observe the waveforms of the input/output signals.

  (a) Set the MODE switch ⑨ to CH1 to display the input signal.

  (b) Adjust the X-axis (time axis) for CH 1 with the TIME/DIV dial ⑥. For example, when the frequency of the signal is 1 kHz, set the TIME/DIV dial to 0.5 ms. Then 5 complete cycles of the signal will be displayed on the screen.

  (c) Confirm that the SWP VAR ⑦ is turned clockwise all the way to the CAL position. Otherwise, the division on the horizontal axis does not match the time interval set by the TIME/DIV dial.

  (d) Set the Y-axis (voltage) for CH1 with the VOLTS/DIV dial ⑫. Set the VOLTS/DIV dial to 0.1 V and adjust the AMPLITUDE knob of the signal generator to 0.2 V.

  (e) Confirm the VAR ⑬ is turned clockwise all the way to the CAL position. Otherwise, each division on the Y-axis does not coincide with the voltage set by the VOLTS/DIV dial.

  (f) Synchronize the sweep. Set the MODE ㉒ to AUTO for the automatic synchronization of the sweep. Set the SOURCE ⑳ to INT and the INT TRIG ㉓ to CH1 so that the sweep is synchronized with the input signal.

(g) Set the AC-GND-DC selector for CH 1 ⑪ to GND to ground the input signal.

(h) Turn on the POWER switch ②. Check the POWER lamp ① is on and wait at least 15 seconds. Then turn the INTENSITY ④ so that the grounded signal (horizontal line) is clearly seen. (Do not make it too bright because it damages the display.) If you cannot see the line, adjust the POSITION knobs ⑭ and ⑧ to adjust the position of the signal in the vertical and horizontal directions.

(i) Turn the FOCUS knob ⑤ to obtain a sharp signal.

(j) Set the MODE switch ⑨ to CH1 to see a sinusoidal signal from the generator. Adjust the position of the waveform with the POSITION knob ⑭ to center the signal.

(k) Set the MODE switch ⑨ to CH2 to display the output signal, and turn the VOLTS/DIV switch for CH2 to 2 V.

(l) Certify that the VAR ⑱ is at the CAL position. If not, the vertical scale of CH2 does not correspond to the voltage set by the VOLTS/DIV ⑰ and you cannot obtain the correct value of the gain.

(m) Set the AC-GND-DC selector for CH2 ⑯ to GND to ground the output signal.

(n) Turn the POSITION knob ⑲ to align the output signal to the X-axis.

11.5.2 Measurement of Frequency Dependence of Gain

1. Measure the frequency dependence of the gain G when the capacitance of the high-pass filter C_H is 3.2 μF and the capacitor in the low-pass filter C_L is OUT.

   (a) Turn on the signal generator and the amplifier.

   (b) Set both of the AC-GND-DC switches for CH1 ⑪ and CH2 ⑯ to AC. The input voltage $\tilde{V}_{in}$ is displayed if the MODE switch ⑨ is set to CH1, and the output voltage is displayed by setting ⑨ to CH2.

   - If the signal does not stop on the screen, adjust the LEVEL knob ㉑ around the center so that the trigger level is within the input signal.

   (c) Set the selector of C_H to 3.2 μF and that of C_L to OUT on the amplifier.

   (d) The change in gain is recognized more easily when input voltage V_{in} is fixed. Adjust the AMPLITUDE knob on the signal generator to set V_{in} to be 0.2 V. Since V_{in} varies depending on the frequency of the input signal, **you need to confirm that V_{in} is 0.2 V every time you change the signal frequency and fine-tune the AMPLITUDE knob as necessary.**

   (e) To measure the frequency dependence of the gain efficiently, first change the frequency coarsely (1 KHz, 100 Hz, 10 Hz, 10 kHz, 100 kHz and 1 MHz) and measure the output voltage V_{out} to get an overall picture.

- Select an appropriate value of the TIME/DIV ⑥ according to the frequency to see the waveform clearly.
- Read the value of V_{out} precisely by positioning the peak of the signal at the Y-axis and using the smallest graduation marks on the axis. When V_{out} is small, adjust the VOLTS/DIV ⑰ to expand the waveform.
- Make sure that the output voltage $\tilde{V}_{out}$ is sinusoidal. If not, either V_{in} is too large or the WAVEFORM switch of the generator is set to be rectangular.

(f) Each time you measure the amplitude of output voltage V_{out}, calculate voltage ratio (voltage gain) V_{out}/V_{in} and power gain in decibel $20\log_{10}(V_{out}/V_{in})$ [dB]. Plot the data on a piece of Semi-log graph paper with a mark such as •.

- It is important to plot a data point each time you make a measurement to grasp the overall shape of the curve and roughly estimate the cutoff frequencies.

(g) Next, measure V_{out} for 30 Hz, 300 Hz, 3 kHz, 30 kH, and 300 kHz. (These are roughly midpoints of the frequencies measured in the previous steps on the logarithmic scale.) Around the cutoff frequency, conduct the measurements more closely. (e.g. 20 Hz, 50 Hz, 70 Hz etc.)

2. Measure the frequency dependence of the gain G when the values of the capacitance in the high-pass filter and low-pass filter are the following: $C_H = 0.8$ μF and $C_L = 820$ pF.

   (a) Set the selector of C_H to 0.8 μF and that of C_L to 820 pF.
   (b) Just as you did in the steps from 1-(a) to 1-(g), measure the amplitude of output voltage V_{out} for various frequencies and plot a gain *vs.* frequency curve for the combination on the same piece of graph paper. Use a different symbol (e.g. ▲) for its data points to distinguish them from the previous set of points for the different combination of the capacitors.

3. Measure the frequency dependence of the gain G for the following combinations of the values of the capacitors: $C_H = 0.165$ μF and $C_L = 3200$ pF.

   (a) Set the selector of C_H to 0.165 μF and that of C_L to 3200 pF.
   (b) Measure the amplitude of output voltage V_{out} for various frequencies and plot a gain *vs.* frequency curve again. Use a different mark (e.g. ■) to show its data points to discriminate them from the previous sets of data points.

11.5.3 Data Analysis

1. For each combination of the filters, obtain the maximum gain $20\log_{10} A_1 A_2$ and the cutoff frequencies f_H and f_L. The maximum gain is given by the value of the flat segment of each graph and the cutoff frequencies are determined

134   CHAPTER 11   FREQUENCY DEPENDENCE OF AMPLIFIER

by drawing a horizontal line 3 dB below the maximum gain and finding the intersections.

2. Using the value of $20\log_{10} A_1 A_2$ obtained in the previous step and given values of R_H, C_H, R_L and C_L, compute the theoretical values of the gain from Equation (11.9) using a spreadsheet program. Plot the results on the graph paper with different symbols (e.g. ○, △ and □) to compare them to your experimental outcomes.

3. Calculate the theoretical values of the cutoff frequency $f_H = 1/2\pi C_H R_H$ and $f_L = 1/2\pi C_L R_L$ for each combination of C_H and C_L and compare the results with the experimental values.

11.6   Comprehension Questions

1. Suppose AC voltage $V_0 \sin \omega t$ is applied to a series RC circuit like the high-pass filter in Figure 11.3. Verify that the voltage across the resistor $\tilde{v}_R$ is given by

$$\tilde{v}_R = \frac{V_0}{\sqrt{1 + \left(\frac{1}{RC\omega}\right)^2}} \sin(\omega t + \phi_R), \qquad \tan \phi_R = \frac{1}{RC\omega}, \qquad (11.11)$$

and that across the resistor $\tilde{v}_C$ is

$$\tilde{v}_C = \frac{V_0}{\sqrt{1 + (RC\omega)^2}} \sin(\omega t + \phi_C), \qquad \tan \phi_C = -RC\omega. \qquad (11.12)$$

2. Show that the amplification of the RC-coupled amplifier approximately increases by 6 dB as the frequency doubles (per octave) in the region below the lower cutoff frequency and decreases by 6 dB per octave for frequencies above the upper cutoff frequency. This rate of decrease in the stopband region is termed *roll-off* or *fall-off*.

3. Discuss practical ways to construct an amplifier that provides a stable gain over as wide range of frequencies as possible.

4. Instead of using a capacitor and resistor, a high-pass filter and low-pass filter can be constructed with an inductor and a resistor (RL filters). Figure out the configurations of such filters and determine their cutoff frequencies.

11.A   Diodes and Transistors

An insertion of a small percentage of impurities such as boron and arsenic, called dopants, into pure (intrinsic) semiconductors like silicon and germanium gives rise to a new type of semiconductors, known as doped (extrinsic) semiconductors. There are two types of doped semiconductors according to its doping agents or majority charge carriers. P-type semiconductors contain trivalent impurities such as boron and aluminum that create deficiencies of valence electrons in the semiconductors, and such deficiencies, called holes, serve as majority charge carriers by accepting electrons from neighboring atoms.[7] On the other hand, n-type semiconductors involve pentavalent impurities like phosphorus and arsenic that donate[8] extra valence electrons to the semiconductors. These extra valence electrons are the majority charge carriers in n-type semiconductors.

Diodes and transistors are circuit elements that consist of different types of semiconductors placed together. A p-n diode is a combination of a p-type semiconductor and an n-type semiconductor and is used as a rectifier, a device that converts alternating current to direct current. Combinations of three semiconductors such as p-n-p and n-p-n are called transistors and they often work as amplifiers. In this section we will describe the mechanisms of rectification and amplification in diodes and transistors.

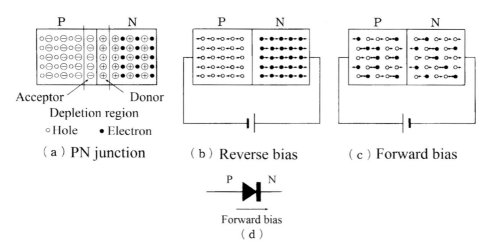

Figure 11.12: Diode. (a) PN junction in equilibrium. A depletion region is formed at the junction. (b) Reverse-biased diode. The driving voltage widens the depletion region. (c) Forward-biased diode. Charge carriers continuously migrate across a narrower depletion region. (d) Circuit symbol of diode. The triangle points in forward-biased direction.

Figure 11.12 (a) illustrates a p-n diode. The interface between the two semiconductors is called a p-n junction. When the junction is formed, some of the electrons in the n-region diffuse into the p-region and combine with holes there, leaving positive donor ions in the n-region and creating negative acceptor ions in the p-region near the junction. These impurity ions are fixed at crystal lattice sites and cannot move. Therefore, these ions constitute an electrical double layer that prevents further diffusion and the diode reaches equilibrium. The electrical layer is known

---
[7] Thus trivalent impurities are called *acceptors*.
[8] Pentavalent dopants are called *donors*.

as a *depletion region*. The potential difference in the region is termed the *potential barrier*, which confines holes in the p-region and electrons in the n-region.

If the positive terminal of a battery is connected to the n-side and the negative terminal to the p-side of a diode as shown in Figure 11.12 (b), the diode is said to be *reverse biased*. In a reverse-biased diode, majority charge carriers are driven away from its p-n junction. This increases the width of the depletion region, and the widened depletion region blocks majority charge carriers.[9] On the contrary, when a higher potential is applied to the p-side than the n-side as in Figure 11.12 (c), majority charge carriers are both pushed toward the junction. As a result, the potential barrier is reduced and the diffusion of majority carriers across the junction resumes. Since charge carriers are replenished by the driving voltage, the process is sustained and a continuous current flows. The diode in this setting is said to be *forward biased*. If a diode is connected to an AC power source, a current flows only when the diode is forward biased. In consequence, AC voltage is converted to DC voltage. This conversion is known as rectification. The circuit symbol for a diode is provided in Figure 11.12 (d).[10]

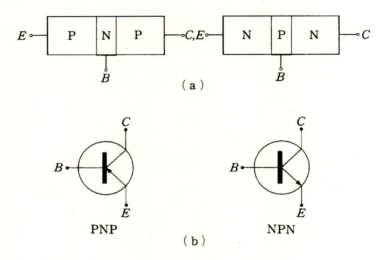

Figure 11.13: Bipolar junction transistors are composed of two p-n diodes. The central region is actually a very thin layer. (a) PNP and NPN transistors. E: Emitter. B: Base. C: Collector. (b) Circuit symbols for PNP and NPN transistors. The arrow points in the direction of the current.

Transistors consisting of a thin doped semiconductor sandwiched by the other type of doped semiconductors are called bipolar junction transistors (BJT).[11] As

---

[9] Minority charge carriers are propelled toward the junction, and a small current still flows in the reverse-biased diode.

[10] In NPN transistors, the flow of majority charge carriers (electrons) is opposite the direction of the arrow.

[11] The first BJT was constructed by William Shockley, John Bardeen and Walter Brattain at Bell Labs in 1947.

shown in Figure 11.13, there are two types of BJT: PNP transistors and NPN transistors. A bipolar transistor has two p-n junction and three terminals are attached to the three regions of the transistor. The terminal attached to the central region is named base (B), the terminals attached to the two end regions are emitter (E) and collector (C) respectively. In a transistor, a small current in the base region regulates larger currents in the end regions. We will explore this current regulation mechanism of PNP transistors.[12]

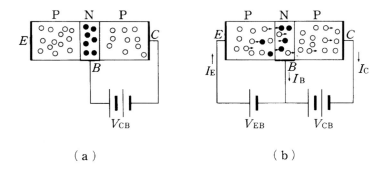

(a)   (b)

Figure 11.14: Charge carriers in a PNP transistor in operation. (a) A high reverse bias voltage V_{CB} creates a wide depletion region/large potential barrier at the base-collector interface. (b) A forward bias voltage V_{EB} drives holes in the emitter region into the base region. The potential barrier at the base-collector interface negatively affects and accelerates the holes and most of the holes enter the collector region. $I_E \approx I_C \gg I_B$.

Without an external voltage applied to a transistor, the potential barriers across the two p-n junctions prevent the migration of majority charge carriers. In operation, the collector-base junction is reverse biased and the emitter-base junction is forward biased. When a reverse bias voltage is applied to the base-collector junction as shown in Figure 11.14 (a), it just increases the depletion region at the base-collector boundary and current hardly flows. However, a forward bias voltage added to the emitter-base junction as in 11.14 (b) decreases the depletion region at the emitter-base junction, and the holes in the emitter region migrate into the base region. Although part of them combines with electrons in the base and make base current I_B, the most part reaches the depletion region between the collector and the base. The depletion region accelerates the holes and the holes flow into the collector, conforming collector current I_C. The value of the applied voltage between the emitter and base V_{EB} regulates the emitter current I_E and the collector current I_C. This is the basic function of transistors. The relationship between I_E, I_B and I_C is

$$I_E = I_B + I_C. \tag{11.13}$$

This equation indicates $I_C/I_E \leq 1$.

---

[12] The same description applies to NPN transistors. The only difference is the type of majority

138 CHAPTER 11 FREQUENCY DEPENDENCE OF AMPLIFIER

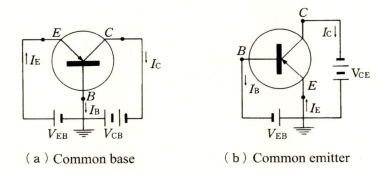

(a) Common base   (b) Common emitter

Figure 11.15: Two commonly used configurations of amplifiers. (a) Common base configuration. $V_{\rm CB}$ provides a reverse bias voltage and $V_{\rm EB}$ regulates the currents. (b) Common emitter configuration. $V_{\rm CE}$ is a reverse bias and $V_{\rm EB}$ works as the current control.

Figure 11.15 indicates two different types of amplifier configurations: Common base configuration or grounded-base configuration (Figure 11.15 (a)) and common emitter configuration or grounded-emitter configuration (Figure 11.15 (b)). One terminal is connected to a common voltage (normally ground) and the other two terminal serve as either an input or output. They are used for different purposes; the former is often used as a current buffer and the latter as an amplifier. Below we will derive a mathematical expression of current gain (current amplification factor) for the common emitter configuration. In general, gain is defined in a differential form:

$$\left(\frac{\partial I_{\rm out}}{\partial I_{\rm in}}\right)_{V_{\rm rev}}, \qquad (11.14)$$

where $I_{\rm out}$ and $I_{\rm in}$ are output and input currents, and $V_{\rm rev}$ is a reverse bias voltage applied to maintain depletion zones in a transistor.[13] For the common base configuration, the emitter current is the input, the collector current is the output. Thus the gain α is defined by

$$\alpha = \left(\frac{\partial I_{\rm C}}{\partial I_{\rm E}}\right)_{V_{\rm CB}}. \qquad (11.15)$$

According to Equation (11.13), α is smaller than one, and it is very close to 1 (typically from 0.9 to 0.99) because of the thinness of the base region. The input and output of a common emitter amplifier are base currents and collector currents.

---

carriers.

[13] Sometimes gain is simply defined in an absolute form: $I_{\rm out}/I_{\rm in}$. However, this definition is not appropriate unless the output is proportional to the input. The two definitions are identical if $I_{\rm out} \propto I_{\rm in}$.

By definition, gain β is

$$\beta = \left(\frac{\partial I_C}{\partial I_B}\right)_{V_{CE}}. \tag{11.16}$$

Since I_C of a common emitter amplifier is regarded as a function of I_B and V_{CE}, we have

$$\Delta I_C = \left(\frac{\partial I_C}{\partial I_B}\right)_{V_{CE}} \Delta I_B + \left(\frac{\partial I_C}{\partial V_{CE}}\right)_{I_B} \Delta V_{CE}. \tag{11.17}$$

However, a small change in a large reverse bias voltage does not affect the output. Therefore, the second term of the right hand side is insignificant. Equation (11.17) is approximated as

$$\Delta I_C \simeq \beta \Delta I_B. \tag{11.18}$$

Likewise, neglecting the derivative of reverse bias voltage V_{CB}, the increment of the collector current for a common base amplifier is

$$\Delta I_C \simeq \left(\frac{\partial I_C}{\partial I_E}\right)_{V_{CB}} \Delta I_E = \alpha \Delta I_E. \tag{11.19}$$

Substituting Equation (11.18) and Equation (11.19) into Equation (11.13), we obtain the relationship between α and β:

$$\beta = \frac{\alpha}{1-\alpha}. \tag{11.20}$$

Since α is close to 1, a large current gain β is achieved in common emitter amplifiers (typically 10 to 100). This is the reason why the common emitter configuration is mostly used in transistor-based amplifiers.

Chapter 12

Absorption of β-Radiation

12.1 Introduction

The discovery of radioactivity in uranium compounds by Henry Becquerel during the last decade of the 19th century opened a new field in physics, nuclear physics. A great deal of research involving radiations has been conducted since then, and these studies have expanded our understanding in nanoscopic or even smaller scales. Although some of the applications of nuclear technology are controversial, the other beneficial usages make the technology crucial to our lives and many scientists and engineers still work in this field. Besides, we need to understand this subject well to assess the benefit and risk of the disputed adaptations of nuclear technology.

In this laboratory we will investigate the absorption of β-particles by metal absorbers with a Geiger counter (G-M tube) to learn interaction between radiations and matters. The principles and characteristics of a Geiger counter will also be studied.

12.2 Objective

1. We will measure the count rate (count per unit time) of β-ray emitted from ^{90}Sr at various voltages applied to a G-M tube. The characteristic curve of the G-M tube will be plotted and its operating voltage will be fixed.

2. Inserting aluminum absorbers of various thicknesses between ^{90}Sr and the G-M tube, we will examine the change in the count rate of β-particles. The resulting absorption curve will be plotted on a logarithmic graph paper. The mass absorption coefficient will be computed from the slope of the graph, and the maximum range and energy of the β-radiation will also be determined from the graph.

12.3 Theory

12.3.1 Radioactive Decay

Radioactive radiations are particles or electromagnetic (EM) waves emitted when an unstable nucleus (radioactive nucleus) decays into another nucleus. Three types of radiations have been identified by Ernest Rutherford and Paul Villard, and they are termed *alpha*, *beta* and *gamma* radiations; α-particles are a $^4_2$He nuclei, β-particles are either electrons or positrons, and γ-rays are highly energetic EM waves.

It has been observed that the mode of radiations and the probability with which a radioactive nucleus decays in a unit time depend on the types of nuclides, and if a radioactive substance contains $N(t)$ nuclei at time t, the number of nuclei ΔN that decay during a small time interval $t \sim t + \Delta t$ is proportional to $N(t)$, i.e. $\Delta N \propto N(t)\Delta t$. Writing it in the form of a differential equation, we obtain

$$\frac{dN}{dt} = -\lambda N(t), \tag{12.1}$$

where λ is *decay constant* (or disintegration constant) characteristic to each radionuclide. Solving the equation yields $N(t) = N_0 e^{-\lambda t}$. Thus the number of remaining radioactive nuclei decreases exponentially. However, ^{90}Sr used in this experiment has a relatively long half-life $T_{1/2}$ (the time it takes for a half of radioactive nuclei to decay) of 29 years, and the number of its radioactive nuclei can be assumed to be constant during several hours of a laboratory activity. The half-life $T_{1/2}$ and decay constant λ of a radionuclide are related as $\lambda T_{1/2} = \ln 2$.

12.3.2 β-Radiation

Highly energetic electrons or positrons emitted during β-decays of radionuclides are called β-radiation. Three types of β-decay are known:

1. β^--decay: A neutron (n) in a radioactive nucleus transforms into a proton (p), emitting an electron (e$^-$) and a neutrino ($\bar{\nu}_e$).[1] (n $\longrightarrow$ p + e$^-$ + $\bar{\nu}_e$)

2. β^+-decay: A proton (p) in a nucleus transforms into a neutron (n), emitting a positron (e$^+$) and a neutrino (ν_e). (p $\longrightarrow$ n + e$^+$ + ν_e)

3. Electron capture: A proton (p) captures an orbital electron (e$^-$) and turns into a neutron (n); a neutrino (ν_e) is emitted during the process. (p+e$^-$ $\longrightarrow$ n+ν_e)

Although β-rays consist both of electrons and positrons in general, we only deal with electrons in this experiment and will call β^--decay simply β-decay. Note that an emission of a β-particle always accompanies with that of a neutrino.[2] Since energy is randomly distributed to an electron and a neutrino during a β-decay, the

---

[1] A neutrino is a very light neutral particle that interacts very weakly with matter. A neutrino emitted during a β^--decay is also called an antineutrino.

[2] The existence of neutrino was first proposed by Wolfgang Pauli in 1930 to explain the conservation of energy and that of momentum in β-decay. The neutrino is a very elusive particle and its observation requires a large-scale detector such as Kamiokande in Hida city, Gifu prefecture. It was finally detected in 1953 by F. Reines and C. L. Cowan.

energy of β-particles is not constant but distributes continuously from 0 to several MeV.[3)]

12.3.3 β-Radiations from ^{90}Sr

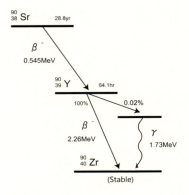

Figure 12.1: Decay mode of ^{90}Sr. After decaying into ^{90}Y, it decays further into a stable ^{90}Zr nucleus.

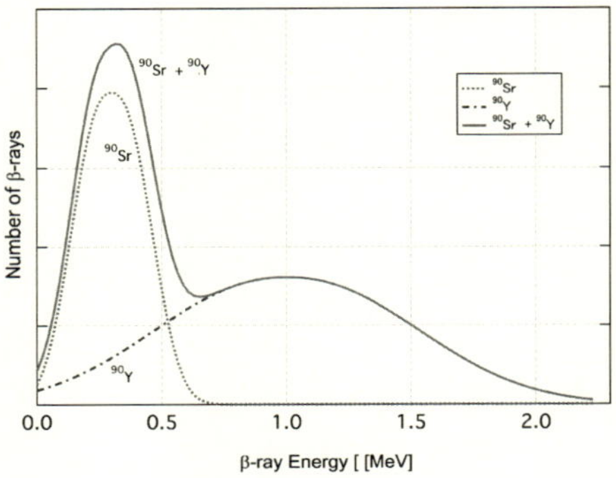

Figure 12.2: Energy spectrum of β-particles from ^{90}Sr. The spectrum consists of β-radiations from ^{90}Sr and those from ^{90}Y.

In this laboratory, we will use ^{90}Sr as a radioactive source, and its decay mode is depicted in Figure 12.1. ^{90}Sr nuclei undergo β^--decays into ^{90}Y nuclei with a half-life of 28.8 years, and they emit β-particles with a maximum energy of 0.545 MeV during the process. Furthermore, ^{90}Y nuclei also undergo β^--decays into a stable ^{90}Zr; its half-life is 64.1 hours and the maximum energy of β-particles emitted during the process is 2.26 MeV.[4)] The β-radiation measured in this experiment is the superposition of β-particles emitted from two different parent nuclei whose spectrum is shown in Figure 12.2. The maximum energy of the spectrum is contributed by the decay of ^{90}Y and its value is $E_{\max} = 2.26$ MeV.

The radioactivity of β-particle sources used in this laboratory is very weak; it is in the order of 10^4 Bq (1 Bq (becquerel) = 1 decay per second).[5)] In addition, each of them is sealed in an aluminum case and then kept in a lead container so that they are handled easily and safely. However, it is advisable not to tamper with them unnecessarily and keep the lid of the container on when they are not used.

[3)] In contrast, in an α-decay a parent radioactive nucleus gives off an α-particle only while decaying into a daughter nucleus, and most of the liberated energy is distributed to the much lighter α-particle. Consequently, kinetic energy possessed by α-particles in a particular mode of decay is a constant.

[4)] 0.02 % of ^{90}Y decays into an excited energy state of ^{90}Zr nuclei, which emit γ-ray to transform into its ground state.

[5)] A biological effect caused by radiation is measured in sieverts (Sv); the biological effect of a radioactive source depends on, obviously, how to treat it.

12.3.4 G-M Tube

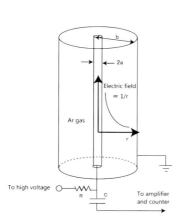
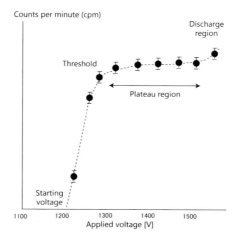

Figure 12.3: A schematic of a G-M tube. Electrons ejected from Ar atoms by a β-particle create a pulse and are recorded as a count.

Figure 12.4: A typical characteristic curve of a Geiger counter. The operating voltage should be selected within the plateau.

A Geiger counter is a device often used to count radioactive particles. It mainly consists of a cylindrical chamber called the G-M tube (Geiger-Müller tube)[6] and a pulse detector. The structure of the G-M tube used in this laboratory is illustrated in Figure 12.3. A conducting wire (tungsten wire) runs along the longitudinal axis of a metal cylinder. The wire and cylinder are electrically insulated, and the former acts as anode (positive electrode) and the latter as cathode (negative electrode). The cylindrical chamber is filled with noble gas (argon) at a pressure about 100 mmHg and polyatomic organic compound (dehydrated alcohol) vapor at 10 mmHg. A high voltage ($\sim$ 1,400 V) is applied between the electrodes. Denoting the radius of the wire as a and that of the cylinder b, the electric field at r from the center of the wire is

$$E(r) = \frac{V}{r \ln(b/a)}. \qquad (12.2)$$

If a charged particle enters into the chamber, it excites or ionizes argon atoms along its path. Electrons emitted from argon atoms are attracted to the positive electrode, and detected as an electric pulse, whereas argon ions collide with alcohol molecules and are neutralized for the G-M tube to restore its original state.[7] The

---

[6] Its principle was first suggested by German nuclear physicist Hans Geiger (1882-1945). Geiger and his Ph.D. student Walther Müller (1905-1979) later developed a practical tube.

[7] These alcohol molecules are called *quenching gas* molecules or *quenchers* because they help stop Ar molecules and quench an electric pulse. Instead of causing further radiations, the energy transferred to quencher molecules is used to dissociate them.

alcohol molecules break down each time an electric pulse is counted, which limits the lifetime of the tube. Our Geiger counters count approximately 10^{10} pulses in total. Avoid setting a measurement time unnecessarily long or fixing the operating voltage too high because it shortens the life of the tube.

For a G-M tube to function properly, an appropriate value of the applied voltage should be chosen. A graph of count rate *vs.* applied voltage (*characteristic curve*) for a G-M tube is shown in Figure 12.4. If the applied voltage is too small, the tube cannot produce an electric pulse large enough to be counted. On the other hand, if the voltage is too high, electric discharge occurs continuously and the radiations are not counted correctly. The range of the voltage where the count rate is approximately constant is called the *plateau*, and the operating voltage should be selected within this range. Since each tube shows a different characteristic curve and the characteristics of the same tube vary with time due to aging, its operational voltage should be determined each time an experiment is conducted.

Not only Geiger counters, a diversity of other types of radiation detectors have been developed so far. Among the most famous are a *cloud chamber* and *bubble chamber* that enabled us to "see" the tracks of the radiation particles incoming into the detectors and led us to discover various new elementary particles. Although G-M counters cannot measure the energy of each radiation particle, proportional counters can measure it by producing an output signal proportional to the energy of incident radiation.

12.3.5 Absorption of β-Radiation by Matter

The absorption of radiation by matter is a consequence of the interaction between the radiation particles and the matter. Electrons incident into a material gradually loses its energy while exciting or ionizing atoms and molecules constituting the substance.[8] Electrons with lower energy are stopped first, whereas those with higher energy transmit a thin material while losing some of their energy. As the thickness of the material increases, more and more electrons are blocked by the matter. This blocking process is interpreted as "absorption". It is experimentally known that the number of β-particles that transmit through an absorber drops exponentially with the thickness of the absorber.[9] If N_0 electrons enters into an absorber of thickness x, the number N of electrons penetrating the absorber is given by

$$N(x) = N_0 e^{-\mu x}, \tag{12.3}$$

where μ defines the **absorption coefficient**. The graph of count rate *vs.* thickness is called the **absorption curve**, and an example of such curves is provided in Figure 12.5. Although electrons with higher energy penetrate thicker absorbers, if the absorber is thick enough, no electron can penetrate the absorber. The minimum

---

[8] Electrons with very high energy (> 10 MeV) lose their energy by *bremsstrahlung* (breaking radiation): electromagnetic radiation emitted from a charged particle when deflected by an electric field produced by atomic nuclei in the matter. The influence of bremsstrahlung is relatively small in this experiment since we will only deal with β-particles of energy up to several MeV.

[9] It reflects the energy spectrum of radiation. Refer to Comprehension Question 2.

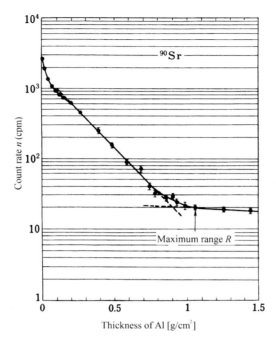

Figure 12.5: β-ray absorption by aluminum plotted on a logarithmic scale. The straight section of the graph indicates an exponential dependence for middle thicknesses (0.2–0.8 g/cm^2). However, the curve digresses from the exponential for thinner absorbers and thicker absorbers due to β-radiation from ^{90}Sr and γ-radiation from ^{90}Y respectively.

value of the absorber thickness that stops all the β-radiation is the *maximum range* (or *end point*) of the β-ray. The electron that reach the maximum range R is the one emitted from the source with the highest kinetic energy $E_{\max}$, and they have one-to-one correspondence. If the maximum energy (end point energy) $E_{\max}$ is expressed in [MeV] and the maximum range in [g/cm^2], they are related as[10]

$$R\,[\mathrm{g/cm^2}] = 0.542 E_{\max}\,[\mathrm{MeV}] - 0.133. \tag{12.4}$$

In Figure 12.5, values of the count rate are not exactly zero for thicknesses larger than R, but approximately take a non-zero constant value. This residual count rate is due to **background radiation**. It is naturally-occurring environmental radiation whose sources include cosmic rays, radioactive materials remaining in rocks and soil, and radioactive isotopes absorbed by plants and passed up in the food chain.

---

[10] Based on the description in L. E. Glendenin, *Nucleonics* 2, 12 (1948). This equation can be applied to β-particles within the range 0.8 MeV $< E <$ 3 MeV. For electrons with energy 0.15 MeV $< E <$ 0.8 MeV, $R\,[\mathrm{g/cm^2}] = 0.407\,(E\,[\mathrm{MeV}])^{1.38}$ fits experimental results better.

146 CHAPTER 12 ABSORPTION OF β-RADIATION

12.4 Apparatus

1. A set of aluminum plates with various thicknesses (used as absorbers).

2. Micrometer (measures the thickness of the absorbers).

3. ^{90}Sr radioactive source (stored in a lead container).

4. G-M tube stand (radioactive sources and absorbers are positioned in it).

5. Radiation counter (Figure 12.6. Model GMS-2T or 3T by OSAKA DEMPA Co.).

    (a) INPUT SELECT: Works as the power switch and mode selector.

    (b) AMP GAIN: Adjusts the amplification of the internal magnifier. Set it to ×1 for this experiment.

    (c) DISCRI: Removes signals smaller a designated magnitude. Set 2–3 for model 2T and $\sim$ 1 for model 3T.

    (d) HIGH VOL: Varies the voltage applied to the G-M tube.

    (e) CONTR(TIMER/MENU): Set it to TIMER to preset the measurement time.

    (f) PRESET TIME: Sets the measurement time.

    (g) RESET: Resets the display to zero.

    (h) START: Starts the measurement. It ends automatically after the time interval designated by the PRESET TIME if the CONTR switch is set to the TIMER.

    (i) STOP: Stops the measurement. No need to use it while using the TIMER.

12.5 Procedure

12.5.1 Functional Check of Radiation Counter

1. After confirming that the HV knob is turned completely counterclockwise to the zero voltage, turn the INPUT SELECT from the OFF position to the TEST position. Check the POWER lamp is on.

2. Set the PRESET TIME to be 1 second, and press the RESET, then START buttons. Verify that the counter stops exactly at 100. If not, repeat this step several times until the display shows 100. If the counting won't stop at 100 after several trials, ask your instructor.

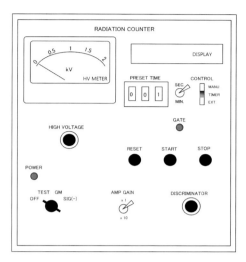

Figure 12.6: The front face of one of the Geiger counters used in the lab.

12.5.2 Determination of Operating Voltage

1. Turn the INPUT SELECT to the GM position. All of the following measurements will be conducted at this position.

2. Remove the lid from the lead container of the radioactive source and place the container with the source at the bottom of the G-M tube stand. Also, put the thinnest Al plate on the tray in the tube. The position of the tray slightly affects your measurements. For the best possible accuracy, set the tray at the second or third position from the top and keep it at the same position throughout the experiment.

3. Set the PRESET TIME to be 1 minute, and press the START to begin the measurement. Then turn the HV knob clockwise to raise the applied voltage until it begins to record events. This is the starting voltage of your Geiger counter (normally 1,000–1,300 V).

4. Within the range between your starting voltage and 1,500 V, measure the counting rate for one minute at various voltages by increasing the voltage by 10 V between the starting voltage and threshold voltage and 50 V in the plateau region. If the count rate exceeds 10 % above the plateau level, stop the measurement to avoid overloading the G-M tube.

5. Plot a count rate *vs.* voltage graph to examine the plateau region. Since our Geiger counters work best at a voltage fairly close to the threshold voltage, choose the voltage at 1/4 of the plateau above the threshold as your operating voltage. In case you did not observe the upper end of the plateau, set 50 V above the threshold as your operating voltage. We will perform the rest of the measurements at this fixed voltage.

12.5.3 Background Radiation

Remove the Al plate and the radioactive source from the G-M tube stand, and the place the lid on the radioactive source container to minimize its influence on the measurement of the background count. Since background counts are relatively small (typically less than 50 counts/minute), you need to measure them longer for better precision. Set the PRESET TIME to be 5 minutes and make a measurement. Calculate the count rate n (counts/min) as the number of counts N divided by the measurement time T. Conduct the same measurement once more after the absorption curve measurement and compute the average value of the background count rate. While waiting, measure the thickness of each aluminum plate with a micrometer.

12.5.4 Absorption of β-Radiation by Al Plates

1. Remove the lid of the radioactive source container and insert it into the G-M tube stand again.

2. Without an Al plate on the tray, measure the count rate for one minute (count rate for thickness = 0).

3. Measure the count rate $n = N/T$ for various thicknesses of the Al plates to construct a count rate *vs.* thickness graph.

    - Plot a data point on a semi-log graphing sheet after each measurement.
    - The thickness x of the Al plates is expressed in [g/cm^2]. It is computed as (thickness in cm) × (the density of Al 2.69 g/cm^3).
    - If the thickest plate is not thick enough to flat out the graph as shown in Figure 12.5, you can superpose two plates.
    - The radioactive decay of atomic nuclei is a random process that obeys the Poisson distribution. According to the Poisson statistics, the uncertainty (standard deviation) for a measured count N is shown to be $\pm\sqrt{N}$. Therefore, each data point of the graph should be represented with an error bar of length $\sqrt{N}/T$. Note that the error $\sqrt{N}$ gets larger as the count value N decreases. (e.g. if a measured count is 10,000, its relative error is $\sqrt{10,000}/10,000 = 1$ %; if a count is 100, then its error is $\sqrt{100}/100 = 10$ %.) This means that we need take the measurement time longer for thicker Al plates to maintain a consistent degree of precision. In this experiment, it is sufficient to make counting rate measurements for 1 minute for thicknesses less than 0.5 g/cm^2, 2 minutes for those between 0.5 and 1 g/cm^2, and 3 minutes for those greater than 1 g/cm^2.

4. Once all the measurements are completed, first turn the HV knob fully counterclockwise to decrease the applied voltage to zero, and then turn the INPUT SELECT to the OFF position to switch off the counter.

12.5.5 Data Analysis

Absorption Coefficient μ

Determine the absorption coefficient μ from the slope of the absorption graph on a logarithmic scale. The number of particles that penetrate an absorber with thickness x in a unit time is given by $n(x) = n_0 e^{-\mu x}$, and it is expressed as a straight line on a logarithmic scale:

$$\log n(x) = \log n_0 - (\mu \log e)x, \tag{12.5}$$

where $\log n$ is the common logarithm $\log_{10} n$. As shown in Figure 12.5, the absorption curve on a logarithmic scale is typically fitted well by a straight line for medium thicknesses whereas it departs from the line for small and large thicknesses. The larger slope at the beginning[11] stems from the fact that β-radiation observed in this experiment originates from two parent radionuclides, ^{90}Sr and ^{90}Y (Figs. 12.1 and 12.2). Thus up to a certain thickness,[12] the absorption curve is the sum of two exponential functions with *two different absorption coefficients*, and it is not a straight line on a logarithmic scale. The slope flattens out at the end as the counts of γ-radiation from ^{90}Y gets more evident. Equate the slope of the fairly straight part of your graph to $-\mu \log e$ to find μ. The absorption coefficient has the unit reciprocal to that of the absorber thickness. In this laboratory, μ has the unit of [cm^2/g] and is termed the **mass absorption coefficient**.

Maximum Range R and Maximum Energy $E_{\max}$

The maximum range R is the minimum thickness of the absorber that blocks all the β-particles. Although the graph deviates from a straight line at large thicknesses and its slope gradually decreases, as long as the slope is not zero, there are still β-particles passing through the absorber. Determine R as the thickness of the absorber where the slope gets almost zero as shown in Figure 12.5.[13] Confirm that the value of the count rate at thickness R roughly agrees with the average value of your measured background count rate. Lastly, using Equation (12.4), compute the maximum energy of the β-particles.

12.6 Comprehension Questions

1. Suppose a 10,000-Bq radioactive source is positioned 10 cm from the circular window of a G-M tube. If the radius of the window is 2 cm, approximately what count rate (cpm) is the Geiger counter expected to detect?

2. Examine the relationship between the energy spectrum of β-radiations and the shape of the absorption curve. If the all the β-particles emitted from a

---

[11] The slope is actually larger if you take the resolving time of the G-M tube into account. Check 12.A Correction for Counting Loss.

[12] See Comprehension Question 3.

[13] Alternatively, one can extrapolate the straight segment and the horizontal segment of the curve (dashed lines in Figure 12.5), and interpret their intersection as R. In this laboratory, however, this method tends to yield a value smaller than the accepted one, 2.26 MeV.

radioactive source have the same energy, what shape would the curve take? Instead, if the energy spectrum is homogeneous from 0 to $E_{\max}$, what would the curve be like?

3. Estimate the maximum range R of β-particles emitted from ^{90}Sr from your absorption curve. It is determined as the thickness of Al at which the initial steeper part of the graph ends and the middle straight portion begins. For better accuracy, it is advisable to correct your graph appropriately using Equation (12.7) first, for the effect of resolving time is more substantial for larger count rates. From the value of R you have obtained, compute maximum energy $E_{\max}$ using[14]

$$E_{\max} [\text{MeV}] = \left(\frac{R \, [\text{g/cm}^2]}{0.407} \right)^{1/1.38}, \qquad (12.6)$$

and check if it agrees with its known value, 0.545 MeV.

12.A Correction for Counting Loss

After a count is recorded in a G-M tube, it requires a certain amount of time to record another count because two particles which enter the tube together or successively within a very small time interval are registered as one pulse. The time interval required to distinct two successive pulses is called the *resolving time*.[15] The resolving time of the Geiger counters used in this laboratory is about 10^{-4} s, and the counting loss due to this resolving time is the major cause for the deviation of the absorption curve from a linear line at high counting rates. Now let's correct this counting loss and derive the true count value N_t.

If the measured count N is recorded for the measurement time T, the "live" measurement time is $T - NT_D$ because the counter is ineffective for T_D after each counting. The true count rate is obtained either using the measured count and the live measurement time or the true count and actual measurement time. We have

$$\frac{N_t}{T} = \frac{N}{T - NT_D}. \qquad (12.7)$$

Thus the true count value after correcting the count loss is given by $N_t = \dfrac{NT}{T - NT_D}$.

---

[14] Refer to footnote 10).

[15] There are three different characteristic time intervals associated to a G-M tube. (a) Dead time T_d: The time interval during which the counter is insensitive to further ionization and unable to make a new pulse. (b) Resolving time T_D: The time interval that has to elapse so that the new pulse is registered as an independent pulse. (c) Recovery time T_r: The time interval needed for the counter to regain its original state. These time intervals satisfy $T_d < T_D < T_r$, and T_D is the most influential on our measurements.

Index

A
absorption, 144
    of beta-radiation, 140, 144, 145, 148
absorption coefficient, 144, 149
    mass, 140, 149
absorption curve, 140, 144, 148–150
AC circuit, 99, 100, 105
acceptor, 135
activation energy, 66, 67, 70
adhesion, 25
adhesive force, 24–26, 31
adiabatic constant, 43, 45, 47
adiabatic process, 43, 45–47, 50
    quasi-static, 43
    reversible, 45
alpha-decay, 142
alpha-particle, 141, 142
alpha-radiation, 141
    spectrum of, 142
alternating current, *see* AC circuit
Ampère's law, 101
amplification, *see also* amplifier
    of diode, 135
    of transistor, 119, 135
amplification factor, *see* gain
amplifier, 118–122, 126, 131, 132, 134, 135, 138, 139
    frequency dependence of, 119
    multistage, 119, 126, 127
    negative feedback, 119–121, 127
    RC-coupled, 118–122, 127, 130, 134
    transistor-based, 139
    vertical, 128, 129
angular frequency, 119, 122
angular momentum, 1, 2, 4–6, 8–11
    conservation of, 1
angular speed, 8–10
angular velocity, 5, 6, 9

anode, 123, 143
    focusing, 127
antineutrino, 141
Avogadro's number, 45

B
Babinet's principle, 64
back emf, 103
background radiation, 145, 148, 149
band theory, 89
base, 136–138
    common, *see* common base
    current, 137, 138
becquerel, 142
Becquerel, Henry, 140
bell, 121
Bell, Alexander Graham, 121
bending moment, 15
beta-decay, 141
    minus, 141, 142
    plus, 141
beta-particle, 140–145, 148–150
beta-radiation, *see* beta-particle
    spectrum of, 142
BJT, *see* transistor
Boltzmann constant, 45, 67, 89
Boyle's law, 47
breaking radiation, *see* bremsstrahlung
bremsstrahlung, 144
bubble chamber, 144

C
calorimeter, 32–36, 41, 42
    water, 33, 36, 39
capacitance, 101, 103
    of high-pass filter, 126, 132, 133
    of low-pass filter, 126, 133
capacitor, 99–101, 103, 105, 107, 108, 110, 111, 113–116, 119, 120,

129, 132–134
    equivalent circuit of, 108
    internal resistance of, 117
capillary action, 25
cathode, 123, 143
cathode ray tube, 122, 123
centroidal axis, 6, 7
ceramic, 108, 111
charge carrier, 135–137
    majority, 135–138
    minority, 136
Clément-Désormes method, 43, 46, 48
Clément, Nicolas, 43
cloud chamber, 144
cohesion, 24
cohesive force, 24–26
coil, *see also* inductor
    self-induction of, 102
collector, 136, 137
    current, 137–139
common base, 138, 139
    gain, 138
common emitter, 138, 139
    gain, 139
complex plane, 106, 107
conduction electron, 66–69, 77, 89
conductivity, 68, 69, 94
conservation law, 1
    of angular momentum, 1
    of energy, 33, 141
constantan, 81
cosmic ray, 145
count rate, 140, 144, 145, 147–150
counting loss, 150
critical nucleus, 85
CRT, *see* cathode ray tube
current density, 68
current distribution, 93, 96
curvature, 22
    center of, 22
    radius of, 14–16, 22, 23
cutoff frequency, 133, 134
    lower, 127
    upper, 122

D

de Broglie wavelength, 64
dead time, 150
decay constant, 141
decibel, 120, 121
degree of freedom, 39

delay angle, 104
depletion region, 135–138
Désormes, Charles, 43
dielectric, 72, 108
    polarization, 108
differential pressure gauge, 48–50
diffraction, 54, 55, 57, 59, 61–64
    2-dimensional, 63
    by hair, 63
    envelope, 61
    factor, 59, 61
    intensity, 59, 61
    multiple-slit, 59, 60, 62
    single-slit, 56, 57, 62
diffraction grating, 55, 59–61, 63, 64
    spacing of, *see* grating constant
diffusion, 79, 89, 135, 136
digital multimeter, 33, 47–49, 84, 95, 96, 113–115
diode, 126, 134–136
    circuit symbol of, 135
    forward-biased, *see* forward bias
    p-n, 135, 136
    reverse-biased, *see* reverse bias
dipole-dipole interaction, 25
disintegration constant, *see* decay constant
DMM, *see* digital multimeter
donor, 135
dopant, 134
doped semiconductor, 69, 134, 136
drift, 67, 82, 89
    speed, 68
    velocity, 68, 89
du Noüy method, *see* ring method
du Noüy, Pierre Lecomte
Dulong-Petit law, 37–39
Dulong, Pierre, 39

E

Eddy current, 107
effective current, 107
effective value, 114
effective voltage, 107, 115
elastic limit, 13
elasticity, 12
    modulus of, 12
electric displacement field, 108
electric field, 90–94, 96, 98
    strength of, 90
electric field line, 90–94, 96–98

property of, 92
electric potential, 90–94, 97
    definition of, 91
electrical double layer, see depletion region
electromagnetic energy, 117
electromagnetic induction, 100, 102
electromotive force, 101
electron, see also charge carrier
    beam, 122
    capture, 141
    gun, 122, 123
electrostatic field, 90, 93, 94, 97
electrostatics, 91
emf, see electromotive force
    induced, 101, 102
emitter, 136–138
    common, see common emitter
    current, 137, 138
endpoint, see maximum range
equipartition theorem, 39
equipotential, 90–93, 96–98
    property of, 92
error bar, 148
excitation, 143, 144
excited state, 142
extensive quantity, 32

F
fall-off, see roll-off
Faraday's law, 102
ferrite, 111
ferromagnetic, 101, 103, 107, 111, 112
field line, see electric field line
flexure, 12, 14, 16, 17, 21
force, see also Newton's second law
    external, 2, 3, 8, 11, 25, 26, 29, 31
    intermolecular, see intermolecular force
forward bias, 135–137
Fraunhofer diffraction, 54, 62, 64
free electron, see conduction electron
free surface, 25, 26
frequency, 118–122, 124, 129, 131–134
    input, 122, 132
Fresnel diffraction, 56
fringe, 55
    bright, see intensity maximum
    dark, see intensity minimum
    missing, see missing order
function generator, see signal generator

G
G-M tube, 140, 143, 144, 146–150
    characteristic curve of, 144
gain, 120–122, 127, 132–134, 138, 139
    current, 138, 139
    frequency dependence of, 122, 132, 133
    in decibel, 120, 122
    maximum, 122, 133, 134
    of feedback amplifier, 122, 127
    power, 120–122, 133
    voltage, 120–122, 133
gamma-decay, 142
gamma-radiation, 141, 149
gamma-ray, 141, 142
gas constant, 45
Gauss' law, 92–94
Geiger, Hans, 143
Geiger-Müller counter, see G-M tube
gimbal, 9–11
grating constant, 55
ground state, 142
grounded-base, see common base
grounded-emitter, see common emitter
gyroscope, 1, 7, 9–11

H
half-life, 141, 142
half-width, 109, 116, 117
harmonic oscillation, 39, 125
He-Ne gas laser, 54
heat, 32, 33
    dissipation, 36
    reservoir, 33–35
heat capacity, 32, 33, 36, 37
henry, 102
high-cut filter, see low-pass filter
high-pass filter, 118, 119, 121, 122, 126, 132–134
hole, 69, 73, 135–137
Huygens, Christiaan, 54
Huygens-Fresnel principle, 54–56

I
ideal gas, 44, 45, 47, 50
    law, 44, 45
impedance, 104–108, 110, 111
    complex, 104, 105, 117
inductance, 103, 112
inductor, 99–103, 105, 107, 108, 110, 111, 113–117

equivalent circuit of, 108
toroidal, *see* toroid
integrating factor, 41, 52
intensity, 55, 57–59, 61–64
factor, 59
maximum, 57, 59, 60, 62
minimum, 57, 58, 61–63
intensive quantity, 33
interference, 54, 55, 61, 62
factor, 59–61
intermolecular force, 24, 30
imbalance of, 24
internal energy, 39
IntuiLink, 33, 35, 49, 84
ionization, 143, 144, 150
isochoric process, 46
isothermal curve, 46
isotropic, 88
isovolumetric process, *see* isochoric process

J
Jolly balance, 27, 28
Jolly, Philip von, 27

K
Kamiokande, 141
kinetic theory, 77
of conduction electron, 66, 88
of gas, 43, 45
Kirchhoff's loop rule, 103

L
LabVIEW, 61–63
leakage current, 108
lever arm, 4
Lissajous figure, 125, 126
Lissajous, Jules-Antoine, 125
Lord Kelvin, *see* Thomson, William
low-cut filter, *see* high-pass filter
low-pass filter, 118–122, 126, 132–134

M
magnetic field strength, 101, 103
main maximum, 59, 60
maximum energy, 142, 145, 149, 150
of beta-radiation, 142
maximum range, 140, 145, 149, 150
Mayer, Julius von, 44
Mayer's relation, 44, 45
mean free path, 66, 77

mean free time, 68, 77
meniscus, 25
concave, 25, 26
convex, 25, 26
micrometer, 28, 29, 146, 148
mirror scale, 28, 29
missing order, 59, 61
mobility, 67–69
molar mass, 37, 76
molar specific heat, 32, 37
electronic, 89
of metal, 39
mole, 32, 39
moment arm, *see* lever arm
moment of force, *see* torque
moment of inertia, 5–7, 9, 11
tensor, 6
Müller, Walther, 143

N
negative feedback, 119
neutral layer, 14–16
neutrino, 141
neutron, 141
Newton's law of cooling, 39–41, 43, 51
Newton's second law, 4
for rotational motion, 1
in angular form, 6
nucleation, *see also* supercooling
heterogeneous, 85
homogeneous, 85, 86
null method, 71
number density, 68, 69, 77

O
Ohm's law, 68, 100, 105
ohmmeter, 71
operating voltage, 140, 144, 147
optical lever, 12, 16
Origin, 50
oscilloscope, 113–116, 118, 122, 123, 125–131
osculating circle, 21, 22

P
p-n junction, 135, 137
parallel *LC* circuit, 99, 110, 116, 117
parallel *RLC* circuit, 106
parallel-axis theorem, 6, 7
passband, 122
Peltier effect, 78, 81

Peltier, Jean Charles, 81
permeability, 102, 111
permittivity, 91, 94, 97
Petit, Alexis, 39
plateau region, *see* operating voltage
platinum resistance thermometer, 33
Poisson distribution, 148
Poisson's law, 45, 47
positron, 141
potential, 90, 96
    barrier, 136, 137
    distribution, 97
    gradient, 93
power loss, 107
precession, 10
primary maximum, *see* main maximum
principal axis, 6
proportional counter, 144
proton, 141
pure semiconductor, 69, 134
P-V diagram, 46

Q

Q factor, 99, 109, 110, 116, 117
quantum effect, 39, 40
quenching gas, 143

R

radiation, 140, 141, 143, 144
    background, *see* background radiation
    counter, 144, 146
radioactive decay, 141, 148
radioactive isotope, 145
radioactive nucleus, 141, 142
radioactive source, 142, 146–150
radioactivity, 140, 142
radionuclide, 141, 149
Rayleigh distance, 62
reactance, 106, 108
    capacitive, 105
    inductive, 102, 105
recovery time, 150
rectangular wave, 125, 130, 133
rectification, 135, 136
rectifier, 135
reduced mass, 46
relaxation time, *see* mean free time
resistance, *see also* Ohm's law
    box, 71, 73
resistivity, 68, 69, 76, 77
    temperature coefficient of, 66, 67, 69
resistor, 70–76, 99–103, 105, 106, 113–115, 119, 120, 126, 134
    variable, *see* rheostat
resolving time, 149, 150
resonance, 99, 108–110, 115–117
    curve, 116, 117
    frequency, 116
    in parallel LC circuit, 110
    in series RLC circuit, *see* series resonance
resonant frequency, 99, 108–111, 116, 117
response time, 50
retrace time, 123
reverse bias, 135, 136
rheostat, 71
rigid body, 1, 2, 4–7
ring method, 24–27
rms current, *see* effective current
rms speed, 88
rms voltage, *see* effective voltage
roll-off, 134
rotational inertia, *see* moment of inertia
rotational motion, 1, 2, 4, 6
    of rigid body, 1, 2, 4
rotor, 9–11

S

secondary maximum, *see* subsidiary maximum
Seebeck coefficient, 79, 80, 86, 87, 89
    absolute, 80
    relative, 79
Seebeck effect, 78, 79, 81
Seebeck, Thomas Johann, 78
self-inductance, 102
semi-log graph, 76, 133, 148
semiconductor, 48, 66, 67, 69, 73, 134–136
    extrinsic, *see* doped semiconductor
    intrinsic, *see* pure semiconductor
    n-type, 135
    p-type, 135
separable equation, 40
series resonance, 109
series RLC circuit, 99, 103, 106–108, 110, 111, 114, 115, 117
SI unit, 21, 26, 33
sievert, 142
signal generator, 132

sinusoidal wave, 100, 105, 118, 119, 121, 122, 124, 125, 131–133
specific gravity, 27
specific heat, 32, 33, 36–39, 44–46
    at constant pressure, 43, 44
    at constant volume, 39, 44, 45
    Einstein's theory of, 46
    molar, *see* molar specific heat
    of gas, 44
    of solid, 32, 37
    ratio of, *see* adiabatic constant
    unit of, 33
spring constant, 30
statistical mechanics, 89
    classical, 89
    quantum, 67, 68, 89
steady current field, 90, 93, 94, 97, 98
stopband, 122, 134
strain, 12–14
    shear, 14
    tensile, 14
stress, 12–14
    compressive, 13
    tensile, 13
subsidiary maximum, 59, 60, 62
supercooling, 85, 86
superposition principle, 91, 93
surface tension, 24–31
    definition of, 25
sweep, 123–125
    sawtooth, 123, 124
    time, 123, 124
    voltage, 124
synchronization, 124

T

temperature data logger, 48
temperature gradient, 78, 82, 87–89
tensiometer, 27
the first law of thermodynamics, 44, 45
thermal emf, 78
thermal vibration, 39
thermistor, 43, 48, 50–52, 66, 69, 72–75
    activation energy of, 66
    carrier density of, 69
    resistance of, 49, 50, 74–76
    thermometer, 48
    time constant of, 51
thermocouple, 78, 81–83
    copper-constantan, 78, 81
    thermometer, 80, 81
thermoelectric effect, *see* Seebeck effect

thermoelectric power, 79, 80
Thomson effect, 78, 81, 82
Thomson, William, 82
threshold voltage, 147
time constant, 40
toroid, 100, 101
torque, 1–6, 8, 10
transistor, 126, 127, 134, 135–138
    bipolar junction, 136
    circuit symbol of, 136
    NPN, 136, 137
    PNP, 136, 137
translational motion, 2, 6
    equation of, 2
    of rigid body, 2
trigger, 124
    level, 124
    negative, 125
    positive, 125

U

unit mass, 33
unit charge, 91

V

van der Waals force, 25
vector field, 90
    conservative, 90
vector triple product, 5
Vernier caliper, 18, 19, 28
voltage, *see also* electric potential
    input, 119–121, 124, 125, 127, 131, 132
    output, 119–122, 132, 133
    thermoelectric, 78, 84

W

wavelet, 54–56, 64
    secondary, 55
    spherical, 56
Wheatstone bridge, 66, 67, 70, 73

X

X-ray diffraction, 64
X-Y oscilloscope, 125, 128

Y

Young's modulus, 12, 13, 15–19, 21
    apparatus, 17

Z

zero method, *see* null method